GRIT AND GRACE

365 TWO-MINUTE DEVOTIONALS

ERIC SPEIR

1

FIRST THINGS MATTER

Seek the Kingdom of God above all else, and live righteously, and he will give you everything you need.
Matthew 6:33

We can be naïve as people because we tend to believe what we hear. If we aren't careful, we will start to believe the lies of the enemy and his lies become our script. Our script then becomes our way of thinking. Our way of thinking becomes our way of behaving. Our way of behaving becomes our life. By now, you get the point.

If you're going to believe everything you hear, you might as well start with the Bible. That's why it's crucial to build a consistent habit of reading God's Word. As we develop the habit of reading God's Word, we can change the way we think (Romans 12:2). That's why first things matter in your day. The promise we have from this Scripture is if we put God first, He'll take care of the rest.

2

DO YOU SEE OPPORTUNITIES OR OBSTACLES?

As soon as the Israelite army saw him, they began to run away in fright. "Have you seen the giant?" the men asked. "He comes out each day to defy Israel. The king has offered a huge reward to anyone who kills him. He will give that man one of his daughters for a wife, and the man's entire family will be exempted from paying taxes!"
1 Samuel 17:24-25

David showed up on the battlefield because he was doing a Grub Hub run for his father. He was there just to deliver some cheese and a few loaves of bread to his brothers. He arrived just in time to see the giant stepping out of the army ranks and cursing God. All the men of Israel ran because they saw an overwhelming obstacle. When others saw an obstacle, David saw an opportunity. Faith will help you see past your current reality to what could be. The key is to keep fighting when others are running.

What obstacle are you facing today that you need to start seeing as an opportunity? Pray and ask the Holy Spirit to give you the courage to face your giant and to have the courage to run toward it.

THE REWARDS OF THE BATTLE

David asked the soldiers standing nearby, "What will a man get for killing this Philistine and ending his defiance of Israel? Who is this pagan Philistine anyway, that he is allowed to defy the armies of the living God?" And these men gave David the same reply. They said, "Yes, that is the reward for killing him."
1 Samuel 17:26

Battles in your life come with a reward. The Bible teaches us that God is the rewarder of those who sincerely seek him (Hebrews 11:6). It's God's nature to give and to reward people (John 3:16). If you're in a battle today, it's not going to be in vain. The greater the battle, the greater the reward. The reward for killing the giant was tax exemption and marrying into the royal family. I don't know about you, but that's a hefty reward! Apparently, it was enough to help motivate David to take on the giant.

Don't be discouraged. If you're fighting a battle in your life, there is a reward just on the other side of your perseverance.

4

DON'T TRADE YOUR TODAY FOR YOUR TOMORROW

"Look, I'm dying of starvation!" said Esau. "What good is my birthright
to me now?"
Genesis 25:32

We live in a microwave culture. We want everything yesterday with no work on our part. In this passage, Esau came in from hunting and was hungry. In a moment of instant gratification, he traded his birthright for a bowl of stew. He gave up his future because he exaggerated his hunger. He said he was dying of hunger. He wasn't dying; he was undisciplined.

To attain what you want in the future, you're going to have to discipline your flesh today. Instant gratification is the enemy of your future. Anything worth having will take time and work. Don't trade what your flesh wants today for your tomorrow.

YOU HAVE A GOOD SHEPHERD

The Lord is my shepherd; I have all that I need.
Psalm 23:1

It's easy to fall into the trap of thinking God is good to everyone but you. This is an excellent passage because David personalizes it for himself. He says, "The Lord is my shepherd." David was going through a difficult season in his life, and he wrote this psalm as a reminder of the goodness of God. Quite often, when I find myself in need, I will quote this psalm out loud to myself. I emphasize that He is my shepherd, and if He is my shepherd, all of my needs will be met. Scripture says faith comes from hearing the word of God (Romans 10:17). The more you hear Scripture the more your faith is built.

Are you in need in some area of your life? If so, try quoting Psalm 23:1 out loud and keep saying it until you believe it.

6

HOLD ON!

Let us hold tightly without wavering to the hope we affirm, for God can be trusted to keep his promise.
Hebrews 10:23

In Greek, the word affirm is *homologia*, which means "the same as" or "to say the same thing." Are your words agreeing with God's Word, or are you in disagreement? When you pray and speak God's Word over your life, you are in agreement with Him. The power of life and death is in the tongue. Be careful what you say.

MAKE IT RIGHT OVER BEING RIGHT

Do all that you can to live in peace with everyone.
Romans 12:18

Conflict is unavoidable in life. We live in a fallen world with other people, and occasionally you're going to be in a disagreement or a conflict. While we may not be able to control every conflict, we can control our response. Most disputes are unresolved because people focus on being right rather than making it right. In this Scripture, the Apostle Paul reminds us to do our part to live at peace with everyone. You cannot control the other person's response, but you can control yours. Always choose peace over being right.

YOU'LL FIND AN EXCUSE, OR YOU'LL FIND A WAY

The lazy person claims, "There's a lion out there! If I go outside, I might be killed!"
Proverbs 22:13

Lazy people look for an excuse while the diligent look for a way. Accomplishing anything of significance in your life is going to take time and hard work. There are no life hacks for this. Don't let excuses keep you from moving forward in your life.

Where are you making excuses about progress in your life? When your why becomes greater than your excuses, you'll find a way.

CHOOSE YOUR SEED

Then God said, "Let the land sprout with vegetation—every sort of seed-bearing plant, and trees that grow seed-bearing fruit. These seeds will then produce the kinds of plants and trees from which they came." And that is what happened.

Genesis 1:11

When farmers plant their fields, they determine their harvest when they choose their seed. A lot of people get frustrated about the harvest in their lives. It's easy to want to blame others around you for the outcomes of your life. The good news is that God gives us the ability to control our harvest by letting us choose our seed.

What kind of seed are you sowing? Are you sowing love or discord? Are you tithing or sowing financial seed? Are you sowing kindness to others? If you don't like your harvest, change your seed. Seed can only reproduce after its own kind.

SECRET PLACES PREPARE YOU FOR PUBLIC SPACES

But David persisted. "I have been taking care of my father's sheep and goats," he said. "When a lion or a bear comes to steal a lamb from the flock, I go after it with a club and rescue the lamb from its mouth. If the animal turns on me, I catch it by the jaw and club it to death. I have done this to both lions and bears, and I'll do it to this pagan Philistine, too, for he has defied the armies of the living God! The LORD who rescued me from the claws of the lion and the bear will rescue me from this Philistine!"
1 Samuel 17:34-37

It might have surprised Saul and everyone else that David could kill a giant, but it was no surprise to David. Why is that? Because David had already killed a lion and a bear in private. David's victory over his private battles gave him confidence in his public battles. David killed the lion and the bear in private before he killed the giant in public. Secret places prepare you for public spaces.

11

DON'T DESPISE PREPARATION

Reaching into his shepherd's bag and taking out a stone, he hurled it with his sling and hit the Philistine in the forehead. The stone sank in, and Goliath stumbled and fell face down on the ground.

1 Samuel 17:49

David's preparation gave him confidence for the battle. Arrogance approaches giants without preparation. When David hit the giant between the eyes with the stone, it wasn't a lucky shot. He had practiced that shot thousands of times before in the sheep field. What David did in secret is what propelled him forward in public.

God uses anointed and prepared people. He also favors the prepared. Don't despise seasons of preparation; you'll eventually get your shot.

12

BLINDED BY CRITICISM

"Do not judge others, and you will not be judged. For you will be treated as you treat others. The standard you use in judging is the standard by which you will be judged. And why worry about a speck in your friend's eye when you have a log in your own? How can you think of saying to your friend, 'Let me help you get rid of that speck in your eye,' when you can't see past the log in your own eye? Hypocrite! First, get rid of the log in your own eye; then you will see well enough to deal with the speck in your friend's eye."
Matthew 7:1-5

We live in a judgmental society. If you're on social media, you'll come to this conclusion quickly. Unfortunately, people will say things behind a keyboard that they would never say in public. If you want to stand out in the world today, then choose to be a person of encouragement.

Before you criticize others, you might take a few minutes for an inventory of your own life. We're not as perfect as we believe ourselves to be. Before you're tempted to criticize someone else, take the time to hear their story. You might be surprised to learn how far they've come.

13

DO IT ANYWAY!

But when David's oldest brother, Eliab, heard David talking to the men, he was angry. "What are you doing around here anyway?" he demanded. "What about those few sheep you're supposed to be taking care of? I know about your pride and deceit. You just want to see the battle!"
1 Samuel 17:28

David's brother Eliab accused him of being conceited. David wasn't arrogant; he was confident. Confidence looks like arrogance to cowards. Don't stop pursuing your vision just because other people don't understand your passion. When you attempt anything significant for God, you'll always have people question your motives. Your courage will reveal their lack of faith. Do it anyway!

START BY DOING THE DISHES

But King Jehoshaphat of Judah asked, "Is there no prophet of the Lord with us? If there is, we can ask the Lord what to do through him." One of King Joram's officers replied, "Elisha son of Shaphat is here. He used to be Elijah's personal assistant."

2 Kings 3:11

Elisha did not start off being known as a great prophet of the Lord. If you go back to his early days, he was plowing fields and doing the work of a hired servant. When Elijah called him to follow him, his only job was to follow Elijah around and serve him. When you read through their story, Elisha did not do one miracle while he was with Elijah. Instead, he was the one who poured water on the hands of Elijah. In other words, he was the one who did the dishes. Don't be afraid to do something that seems beneath you. If you want to be an Elisha, you might have to start by doing the dishes.

15

DON'T BE TOO GOOD TO CARRY THE GROCERIES

One day Jesse said to David, "Take this basket of roasted grain and these ten loaves of bread, and carry them quickly to your brothers. And give these ten cuts of cheese to their captain. See how your brothers are getting along, and bring back a report on how they are doing."
1 Samuel 17:17-18

Don't be afraid to do something that seems beneath you. David carried groceries to the battlefield and ended up defeating a giant. His obedience led to his opportunity. A lot of people miss opportunities because they lack obedience. If God can't trust you with something little, he can't trust you with something big. God will not give you a big opportunity if he can't trust you to do what's in front of you.

KEEP PUTTING IN THE WORK

Sanballat was very angry when he learned that we were rebuilding the wall.
He flew into a rage and mocked the Jews, saying in front of his friends and the
Samarian army officers, "What does this bunch of poor, feeble Jews think
they're doing? Do they think they can build the wall in a single day by just
offering a few sacrifices? Do they actually think they can make something of
stones from a rubbish heap—and charred ones at that?"
Nehemiah 4:1-2

When Nehemiah and the remnant of Jerusalem decided to rebuild the walls of the city, they faced overwhelming odds. Their enemies were set on destroying them and impeding progress any way they could.

Our enemy is no different. He will do anything he can to destroy your life (John 10:10). I want to encourage you to flip the script in your life. The enemy's opposition to your life is evidence of your potential. He's scared of what you're capable of! Don't let it discourage you; let it fuel you. Keep putting in the work.

17

THE PRAYER CLOSET

But when you pray, go away by yourself, shut the door behind you, and
pray to your Father in private. Then your Father, who sees everything,
will reward you.
Matthew 6:6

The secret sauce for Jesus' ministry was His prayer life. Jesus often withdrew to a lonely place to pray (Luke 5:16). We live in a world where everyone is looking for the next life hack or shortcut. There's no life hack for spiritual vitality. The secret is the secret place.

In my early years, my morning commute was my prayer closet. Years later, it's my living room. Either way, find something that works for you and pray.

18

YOU HAVE RIGHTS

You say, "I am allowed to do anything"—but not everything is good for you. And even though "I am allowed to do anything," I must not become a slave to anything.
1 Corinthians 6:12

Paul was writing to the Corinthian church, which was struggling with the idea of doing their own thing and living for themselves. Not much has changed. We live in a culture where, with little regard for anyone else, we do what we want to do. For the believer, we have been called to live at a higher standard than everyone else.

As a father and pastor, I am keenly aware that people are watching me and paying attention to my life. I don't want to do anything to damage the Lord's reputation or to lead someone down the wrong path.

Just because you can, it doesn't mean you should. Some things are beneath the dignity of your calling.

19

FAITH OVER FEAR

Don't be afraid, for I am with you. Don't be discouraged, for I am your God. I will strengthen you and help you. I will hold you up with my victorious right hand.
Isaiah 41:10

Faith and fear have two things in common. They both want to predict your future, and they're both a choice. The spirit of fear wants you to choose lies and get you to believe things that have not happened. On the other hand, faith chooses to believe God is with us and will help us. The choice is yours. Choose wisely!

20

IT'S WORTH THE WAIT!

Now Sarai, Abram's wife, had not been able to bear children for him. But she had an Egyptian servant named Hagar. So Sarai said to Abram, "The LORD has prevented me from having children. Go and sleep with my servant. Perhaps I can have children through her." And Abram agreed with Sarai's proposal.
Genesis 16:1-2

As a result of Abraham and Sarah's impatience, they birthed Ishmael. In essence, he was their shortcut to the promise of God. There are no short-cuts when it comes to waiting on God.

Waiting is not easy. The only thing worse than waiting is wishing you had. It's better to wait than to regret. If you're waiting on God, it's best to keep waiting.

21

DON'T FALL FOR THE TRAP

Oh, don't worry; we wouldn't dare say that we are as wonderful as these other men who tell you how important they are! But they are only comparing themselves with each other, using themselves as the standard of measurement. How ignorant!
2 Corinthians 10:12

Don't fall into the comparison trap, especially the one we see on social media. Most often, you're viewing someone's highlight reels rather than their struggles. Stay the course and find contentment in your life. Gratitude is the answer. The best way to avoid comparing yourself to others is to be thankful for what you have and for who God made you to be.

22

STRUGGLE ON!

So let's not get tired of doing what is good. At just the right time we will reap a harvest of blessing if we don't give up.
Galatians 6:9

It's time we flip the script on struggling. Too many times, we feel like we are failing if we are struggling. The only people who don't struggle are dead people. If you're not struggling, you're not trying. Only people who pursue progress face struggles. Struggle on!

23

LIONS AND TIGERS AND BEARS, OH MY!

But David persisted. "I have been taking care of my father's sheep and goats," he said. "When a lion or a bear comes to steal a lamb from the flock, I go after it with a club and rescue the lamb from its mouth. If the animal turns on me, I catch it by the jaw and club it to death. I have done this to both lions and bears, and I'll do it to this pagan Philistine, too, for he has defied the armies of the living God!"
1 Samuel 17:34-36

When David faced Goliath, it was the first time he ever met a giant. However, it wasn't the first time he ever faced anything life-threatening. He had already been tested with a lion and a bear and had prevailed.

David's past victories gave him confidence for today's problems. A promotion came to David's life, but it only came after he killed the giant. Problems in today's season qualify you for your next season. Don't run from what is meant to equip you for the next level.

24

REVERSE THE CURSE

So the floodwaters gradually receded from the earth. After 150 days, exactly five months from the time the flood began, the boat came to rest on the mountains of Ararat.
Genesis 8:3-4

Noah and his family went through a time of destruction and turmoil. It was a long and challenging season, but they rode it out. The ark eventually came to rest on Mount Ararat. In Hebrew, Ararat means "reverse the curse."

We've just come through a tough season that has brought destruction, but I'm trusting the Lord to "reverse the curse" and turn things around for our good. God didn't bring us this far just to bring us this far.

Where do you need God to reverse the curse in your life? Ask him right now to reverse what's been cursed in your life.

25

YOU'RE NOT QUALIFIED

You didn't choose me. I chose you. I appointed you to go and produce lasting fruit, so that the Father will give you whatever you ask for, using my name.
John 15:16

Have you ever felt like you weren't qualified to do something, especially something God called you to do? I hate to break it to you, but you're probably right. You're not qualified, but you are chosen. God chose you before you chose Him. Quit feeling like you're not qualified and go do what the Lord has told you to do.

WHEN PREPARATION MEETS OPPORTUNITY

*"Then the Kingdom of Heaven will be like ten bridesmaids who took
their lamps and went to meet the bridegroom. Five of them were foolish,
and five were wise. The five who were foolish didn't take enough olive
oil for their lamps, but the other five were wise enough to take along
extra oil. When the bridegroom was delayed, they all became drowsy
and fell asleep."*
Matthew 25:1-5

In this parable, only half of the bridesmaids were prepared. The five
foolish ones did not bring enough oil, while the wise ones brought extra.
The wise ones were prepared for their opportunity. Preparation precedes
opportunity. If you wait to prepare after the opportunity, it's too late.
Opportunities are missed because of a lack of preparation.

27

CHARACTER MATTERS

*But the L*ORD *said to Samuel, "Don't judge by his appearance or height,*
*for I have rejected him. The L*ORD *doesn't see things the way you see*
*them. People judge by outward appearance, but the L*ORD *looks at the*
heart."
1 Samuel 16:7

We live in a culture where people value charisma over character. This
was a problem in biblical days as it is now. King David wasn't there for
draft day with his brothers. He wasn't Samuel's first pick. In fact, he was
the last pick. He was number eight! However, God had already chosen
David, so it didn't matter where he was picked. It's our job to focus on our
character. It's God's job to focus on our pick.

GET OUT OF YOUR BOAT

Then Peter called to him, "Lord, if it's really you, tell me to come to you, walking on the water." "Yes, come," Jesus said. So Peter went over the side of the boat and walked on the water toward Jesus.
Matthew 14:28-29

Peter gets a bad rap in Scripture. Sure, he constantly put his foot in his mouth and was short-tempered, but the man was passionate. When the disciples were in a boat, and Jesus was walking on water toward them Peter was the only one to get out of the boat.

Are you holding back somewhere in your life? Are you afraid to take a step of faith and trust God with part of your life? If so, take a small step today and see what happens. If it were easy, everyone would do it. What you want most is just beyond your comfort zone.

29

TEMPORARY SILENCE

Then they went home and prepared spices and ointments to anoint his body.
But by the time they were finished the Sabbath had begun, so they rested as
required by the law.
Luke 23:56

The day between the crucifixion and the resurrection was a day of silence. Hell was rejoicing, the disciples were hiding, and the women were weeping. It looked like all hope had been lost. However, the silence was temporary because Sunday was coming!

Every believer faces times when they do not hear anything from God. You might feel like God has abandoned you. Just because you don't see anything happening, doesn't mean God's not working. God does His best work in silence. When you feel abandoned, you have to press into the truth of God's Word, knowing that "He will neither fail you nor abandon you" (Deut. 31:8). You might not be hearing anything today, but Sunday is coming!

30

ONE BAD DAY

The faithful love of the L<small>ORD</small> *never ends! His mercies never cease. Great is his faithfulness; his mercies begin afresh each morning.*
Lamentations 3:22-23

Jesus died on the cross over 2000 years ago. To say He had a bad day would be a gross understatement. He died, but on the third day, He rose again. We all have bad days. You might be having a bad week or a bad month, but we must remember that God is faithful; and He's merciful to us.

Just like Jesus, one bad day doesn't decide your future. If your name was on the wake-up list this morning, you can rejoice at God's mercy, knowing He still has something for you to do. No matter what problems or difficulties you're facing, you can hold fast to the promise that God always gets the last word! Hell thought they had won, but on the third day, Jesus rose again.

31

WHO IS IN YOUR CIRCLE?

But Rehoboam rejected the advice of the older men and instead asked the opinion of the young men who had grown up with him and were now his advisers.
1 Kings 12:8

If you're the smartest one in your circle, you need a bigger circle. Unfortunately, Rehoboam surrounded himself with people just like himself. They would tell him what he wanted to hear rather than the truth. Not only did they not give good advice, but they also lacked the experience to understand what needed to be done.

There's nothing wrong with having young people who think differently on your team. We need people of different generations in our lives and with different experiences, but we also need some gray-haired people who have fought some battles and have lived to talk about it. Experience is a good teacher, if you will listen.

32

IT'S NOT EASY, BUT IT'S POSSIBLE!

Jesus looked at them intently and said, "Humanly speaking, it is impossible. But with God everything is possible."
Matthew 19:26

We have our limits. We can only do so much. Even though we have limitations, God does not. Scripture says He has no beginning and no end (Hebrews 7:3). God is without limits. Sometimes it's easy to forget this fact. Our role is to have faith. God's role is to do the impossible.

Faith makes things possible, not easy. What are you facing that's impossible with man, but possible with God?

33

IN THE BEGINNING

In the beginning God created the heavens and the earth.
Genesis 1:1

In the beginning the Word already existed. The Word was with God, and the Word was God.
John 1:1

How you begin matters. In the book of Genesis, God spoke everything into existence with the Word. In the Gospel of John, He started with the Word again.

Start your day with a new commitment to God's Word. The Word has the power to transform your life into what it was meant to be. He started with the Word, so should we!

GOING THE EXTRA MILE

If a soldier demands that you carry his gear for a mile, carry it two miles.
Matthew 5:41

In this passage, Jesus was encouraging His disciples to do more than what the Law required. According to Roman law, if a Roman soldier commanded a Jew to carry his gear for one mile, the person was required to carry the gear for one mile.

As believers, we should be the two-mile people. We should strive to do more than the minimum, especially on our jobs and in our relationships. If you want to land a promotion, start going the extra mile. We should have the best attitudes and be the hardest working people on our jobs. If you want better relationships, start going the extra mile. Don't be afraid to go the extra mile; there's no competition.

35

LOSING THE POPULARITY CONTEST

And what do you benefit if you gain the whole world but are yourself lost or destroyed?
Luke 9:25

In an Instagram and TikTok-driven world, people will often do anything they can to become famous. It's shameful to think of how much someone will do or show on social media just to get a Like or a Share. Somehow, we've bought into the idea that being popular will help us gain more out of life. We must be careful as believers and remember we can have it all and still have nothing.

Just because someone is famous, doesn't mean they're right. Don't be swayed by popular opinion.

36

KEEP YOUR WORD

But if you fail to keep your word, then you will have sinned against the LORD,
and you may be sure that your sin will find you out.
Numbers 32:23

In this passage, Moses reminded the tribes of Reuben and Gad to keep their commitment to the rest of Israel. Their plan was to settle down on one side of the Jordan while the other tribes crossed over and possessed their portion of the land. Their promise was that if they could have that portion, they would cross over and help the other tribes possess their share.

We live in a culture that makes a lot of commitments but lacks follow-through. We trust charisma over character. You can fake charisma, but you can't fake character. It will eventually expose you. Following through on your word is how you build a good reputation. Not following through on your commitment is how you lose your reputation. The good news is that it's your choice!

CHOOSING YOUR SEED

Don't be misled—you cannot mock the justice of God. You will always harvest
what you plant.
Galatians 6:7

I've never met a farmer who was surprised by his harvest. Why is that? Because you choose your harvest when you choose your seed. When a farmer plants corn, he knows he's going to get corn. When he plants carrots, he knows he's going to get carrots. There are no surprises for him. The only surprise he gets is the size of the harvest because the potential of the harvest is in the seed. You can count the number of seeds in an apple, but you cannot count the number of apples in a seed. Seed determines harvest.

On a more practical note, I often give believers this reminder: you are free to choose, but you are not free from the consequences of your choices. You reap what you sow. Choose wisely.

38

ASK FOR ADVICE

Plans go wrong for lack of advice; many advisers bring success.
Proverbs 15:22

Don't be too prideful to ask for advice. The Titanic didn't sink just because of an iceberg. It sank because the captain ignored the wise counsel of others to sail around the icebergs.

Asking for advice is hard. Learning from mistakes is hard. Choose your hard.

39

DON'T PROCRASTINATE

Then the king told Amasa, "Mobilize the army of Judah within three days, and report back at that time." So Amasa went out to notify Judah, but it took him longer than the time he had been given.

2 Samuel 20:4-5

In this passage, Amasa was given a dream assignment by the king. His only requirement was to gather the troops for battle and report back to the king in three days. For whatever reason, Amasa took longer than the king allotted. It's my opinion that he procrastinated. Every door of opportunity has an expiration date. Delayed obedience and procrastination are the biggest culprits to missed opportunities.

If you've procrastinated or delayed on the King's command in your life, then repent and get moving. He has a God-given assignment for you, but it's going to require you to put on your work boots and get to work. If you cannot see the whole way forward, just do the next right thing. After you do that, do the next right thing.

40

TRUST THE LORD

Trust in the Lord *with all your heart; do not depend on your own understanding.*
Proverbs 3:5

I must confess something to you. I have trust issues. I have a hard time trusting people, so I often have a hard time trusting God. Over the years, it's taken me time to trust the Lord and not rely on myself or my own way of thinking. Truthfully, it is a daily battle.

I want to encourage you to always trust God's character and abilities more than your circumstances. Your circumstances and emotions will lie to you; God will not. Lying is against His nature. Thus, you can trust His Word and lean on it.

41

STEP INTO THE WATER

It was the harvest season, and the Jordan was overflowing its banks. But as soon as the feet of the priests who were carrying the Ark touched the water at the river's edge, the water above that point began backing up a great distance away at a town called Adam, which is near Zarethan.
Joshua 3:15-16

When Joshua was leading the Israelites to cross the Jordan River, the instructions from the Lord were to step into the water (at flood stage, mind you!), and then it would part.

It takes faith to step before you see the miracle. We often want God to do the supernatural before we do the natural. Unfortunately, that's not the way it works. Where is God asking you to take a step of faith? You must step into the water before the water will part. Faith requires work.

TAKE CARE OF TODAY

*Then Joshua told the people, "Purify yourselves, for tomorrow the Lord
will do great wonders among you."*
Joshua 3:5

Israel's job was to prepare for the miracle; God's job was to do the miracle. We do the natural; He does the supernatural. We do the natural by consecrating ourselves to the Lord.

Consecrate means to make holy or to set oneself apart to God. How do we consecrate ourselves to the Lord? We consecrate ourselves to the Lord by praying and ensuring our hearts and hands are clean before Him. When we do this, He'll do the rest.

43

DIG THE DITCHES

*While the harp was being played, the power of the L*ORD *came upon Elisha, and he said, "This is what the L*ORD *says: This dry valley will be filled with pools of water!"*
2 Kings 3:15-16

The armies of Israel, Judah, and Edom banded together to fight the Moabites. It was an unusual trio for sure, for they were unequally yoked in their relationship with the Lord. They were marching through the desert because it was the quickest route, but they ran out of water. They were dying of thirst. Finally, someone got the bright idea to ask a prophet for the Lord's help.

When you don't know what else to do, pray. I would encourage you to always pray first, but that's another devotional. Elisha prophesied to them that the Lord would come through and provide water for them. This was going to be a spectacular miracle for sure, but it would require them to dig ditches.

Everyone wants abundance to flow; few people want to dig ditches. Dig the ditches, then the water will come. You've been asking for provision, but the Lord might just be waiting on you to dig the ditches first. Provision favors the prepared.

44

DON'T BE DESTROYED

My people are being destroyed because they don't know me. Since you priests refuse to know me, I refuse to recognize you as my priests. Since you have forgotten the laws of your God, I will forget to bless your children.

Hoses 4:6

This is a sobering truth for the Church. We are being destroyed because we don't know who God is. His desire is for us to know Him and to be in fellowship with Him. When we don't know God, we don't know His Word. When we don't know His Word, we become like the world.

When I was courting my wife, we spent a lot of time together. I would give up sleep just to talk with her on the phone and to hear her voice. The more I knew her, the more intimate we became. Eventually, our courting led to our marriage. We would never want to marry someone without spending time together. That's why having a daily prayer and Bible reading habit is essential. You can never know God without spending time with Him.

45

DON'T RETURN TO THE VOMIT

As a dog returns to its vomit, so a fool repeats his foolishness.
Proverbs 26:11

At some point, everyone is going to do something stupid. The book of Proverbs refers to this as being foolish. It's one thing to do something foolish; it's another thing to repeat it. The first time it was a mistake. The second time it was a choice.

Mistakes are only wasted when you refuse to learn the lessons. If you've made a mistake, repent, learn the lesson, and move on. Whatever you do, don't dwell on it, and don't return to it.

46

SPEAK TO YOUR MOUNTAIN

Then Jesus said to the disciples, "Have faith in God. I tell you the truth, you can say to this mountain, 'May you be lifted up and thrown into the sea,' and it will happen. But you must really believe it will happen and have no doubt in your heart. I tell you, you can pray for anything, and if you believe that you've received it, it will be yours."
Mark 11:22-24

God spoke the world into existence with His words. Simply put, His word changes things. The Bible also declares that the power of life and death are in the tongue. When Jesus was facing an overwhelming storm in His life, He rebuked the storm. He didn't beg or negotiate with it. He simply used His words to rebuke it.

Jesus expects His disciples to do the same because He gave us all the authority we need. How do we speak to our mountains? By speaking life over our problems. We do this when we speak the Word of God over our situations. If you're sick, then you need to confess Scriptures that relate to healing. If you need provision, you need to speak Scripture that relates to God's abundance and provision. By now, you get the point.

You're one prayer away from a different outcome. Don't give up; keep speaking to your mountain.

47

SURVIVING YOUR WILDERNESS

Then Jesus, full of the Holy Spirit, returned from the Jordan River. He was led by the Spirit in the wilderness, where he was tempted by the devil for forty days. Jesus ate nothing all that time and became very hungry.
Luke 4:1-2

It's sobering to think the Holy Spirit was the one who led Jesus into the wilderness. Jesus was not there because of sin or disobedience. He didn't do anything wrong; He did everything right.

If you're in a wilderness today, it could be that God is wanting to do something new in your life. Wildernesses are not permanent. They're transitions to your next season. It's a tough season where the Holy Spirit will take you to a new level of trust in Him. The Holy Spirit will never lead you to a place where He cannot sustain you.

THE BEST IS YET TO COME!

When the master of ceremonies tasted the water that was now wine, not knowing where it had come from (though, of course, the servants knew), he called the bridegroom over. "A host always serves the best wine first," he said. "Then, when everyone has had a lot to drink, he brings out the less expensive wine. But you have kept the best until now!"
John 2:9-10

If you watch the news too much, you'll end up depressed. If we aren't careful, we'll buy into the lie that things are too far gone, and there's nothing else God can do. The older we get, the easier it is to think the best days are behind us.

When I was younger, I would hear people refer to the "good ole days." I'm thankful for the good ole days, but I don't want to go back there. I want to press into what God wants to do in my life and in the future. This verse reminds us that God has "kept the best until now!" The Lord has saved his greatest outpouring for now. Our best days are ahead of us, not behind us. The best is yet to come!

DON'T KID YOURSELF

"If you are faithful in little things, you will be faithful in large ones. But if you are dishonest in little things, you won't be honest with greater responsibilities."
Luke 16:10

Don't be fooled; little things matter. Too many people fool themselves into thinking they'll start tithing and giving when they have more. If you won't tithe on what you have, you won't tithe on what you want. The best way to be trusted with much is to be trusted with a little.

I wasn't always a giver, but over the past several years, I've been praying and asking God to help me to be more generous. I'm not perfect, but I'm more generous than when I first started serving the Lord. I've learned to overcome this by slowly building trust with the Lord.

I've also made it a point to get better at being a better steward of my finances by trying to get out of debt. It's not easy, but it's worth it.

DON'T BE TOO HASTY

Enthusiasm without knowledge is no good; haste makes mistakes.
Proverbs 19:2

Enthusiasm and passion in life are essential. Without passion, you'll never accomplish anything of significance. It's what will get you out of bed in the morning. Passion will also keep you going when you feel like quitting. However, passion is not enough. You'll need the knowledge to go along with it. Without knowledge, you'll make bad decisions.

I've made many bad decisions over the years, but I'm thankful for mentors and books. With their help, I've done a better job of making decisions. Making bad decisions is hard. Learning from someone else is hard. Choose your hard.

DON'T BE LAZY

Lazy people want much but get little, but those who work hard will prosper.
Proverbs 13:4

Everyone wants to prosper; few people want to work. Self-discipline is the biggest obstacle between you and your dreams. The secret sauce of prosperity is the blessing of God and hard work. Thomas Jefferson once said, "The harder I work the luckier I get." I don't think success is about luck, but there's a correlation between those who work hard and those who push past the obstacles.

It's easy to envy the success of others and think their life has been a bed of roses. Over the past few years, I've been more intentional about hearing other people's stories, especially the stories of successful people. One thing they've all had in common is that they've had to work hard and overcome overwhelming odds. Amidst that, they've seen the blessing of God on their lives. If you stay at something long enough, you'll find success.

52

DON'T PROCRASTINATE

Remember, it is sin to know what you ought to do and then not do it.
James 4:17

The Apostle James holds nothing back in this verse. He comes out swinging with no gloves on. He states that to know what to do and not do it is a sin. Is he saying that to keep intentionally procrastinating on something a sin? Yes, he is! Delayed obedience is still disobedience.

This is a hard pillow to swallow as over the years, I have procrastinated for various reasons. I'm not perfect, but I'm getting better. To overcome this, I've learned to apply the principle of doing the worst first. To do the worst first is to do the hardest things first and get them out of your way. Doing this builds confidence in your abilities, and you make the rest of your day easier. To beat procrastination, you must to do the worst first.

What has God told you to do that you haven't started doing yet? Don't delay; get started today! (That last line sounds like a corny car salesman, doesn't it?)

THE RIGHT THING IN THE WRONG SEASON

Now David's son Absalom had a beautiful sister named Tamar. And Amnon, her half-brother, fell desperately in love with her. Amnon became so obsessed with Tamar that he became ill. She was a virgin, and Amnon thought he could never have her.
2 Samuel 13:1-2

This story does not end well. Amnon was in love with his half-sister Tamar. At the end of the story, Amnon rapes his half-sister, Tamar. Truthfully, he wanted love and sex. In the confines of the marriage covenant, there is nothing wrong with either of these desires. He devised a plan to bring her to his house and then sleep with her. This was the wrong way to go about finding fulfillment in a relationship. He should have asked his father if he could marry her. I doubt David would have refused him. This was a case of the right thing in the wrong season.

The right thing in the wrong season can destroy you. Don't rush things in your life. Sometimes God makes you wait to protect you. If there is something you're wanting, take the time to ask your Father. He's good about giving good gifts to His children.

54

FAVOR FOLLOWS WORK

"I hope I continue to please you, sir," she replied. "You have comforted me by speaking so kindly to me, even though I am not one of your workers."
Ruth 2:13

The story of Ruth is a great one. People love this story because Ruth was favored by God to marry the richest bachelor in town. She would also later give birth to the great grandfather of King David and be in the family line of the Messiah. That's a great ending to her story!

What most people miss about this story is that at the beginning, she had to go out into the fields and pick up the leftovers after the harvesters. She did this for the wheat and barley harvests, which were two different seasons. She likely did this for about a year.

If you want to attract the favor of God on your life, you need to put in the work. It's not that you're working for it, but God's favor usually rests on those who are doing something for others. In this case, Ruth was working to support herself and her mother-in-law.

One last thought. You can be in the right place at the right time, but if you don't have the work ethic, you may not get what the Lord wants for you.

THE KEY TO TRANSFORMATION

Don't copy the behavior and customs of this world, but let God transform you into a new person by changing the way you think. Then you will learn to know God's will for you, which is good and pleasing and perfect.

Romans 12:2

I can say with confidence that the single most transformational habit I've developed over the years is the daily reading of God's Word. There's simply no better way to grow in your relationship with the Lord. It has been the key to transforming my mind and helping me to become more like Christ.

I would also add, it is the only way to know the will of God for your life. The more I read the Word of God, the more His will has become clear to me. You cannot know God's will for your life apart from a personal relationship with Him. There are no shortcuts for this. The Word of God is the will of God for you.

56

DON'T BE AFRAID TO REPEAT

"There was a judge in a certain city," he said, "who neither feared God nor cared about people. A widow of that city came to him repeatedly, saying, 'Give me justice in this dispute with my enemy.' The judge ignored her for a while, but finally he said to himself, 'I don't fear God or care about people, but this woman is driving me crazy. I'm going to see that she gets justice, because she is wearing me out with her constant requests!'"
Luke 18:2-5

Praying is hard work. For years, I would allow the enemy to beat me up over my lack of prayer or my lack of not knowing what to say. On many occasions, I would find myself praying for the same things. At times I felt like I was probably disappointing God for this. Have you ever felt like this?

After reading this verse, it clicked in my spirit. According to this passage, we can and should repeat our requests to the Lord. Some things in your life just take time. Don't feel bad for repeating the same prayers every day. If it's worth praying, it's worth repeating!

IT'S GOING TO GET MESSY

Without oxen a stable stays clean, but you need a strong ox for a large harvest.
Proverbs 14:4

The farmer understands that if he is going to have a harvest, he needs an ox to plow the ground. You can either have perfection or progress, but you can't have both. You can't have a harvest without a bit of manure. Life is rarely perfect, and things often get messy.

My wife and I have four children, and our house rarely stays clean for long. For years it drove me bonkers, but I've concluded that I would choose to have children over a perfect home. Always choose progress over perfection.

JUST KEEP SWIMMING, JUST KEEP SWIMMING!

"And so I tell you, keep on asking, and you will receive what you ask for. Keep on seeking, and you will find. Keep on knocking, and the door will be opened to you. For everyone who asks, receives. Everyone who seeks, finds. And to everyone who knocks, the door will be opened."
Luke 11:9-10

In the iconic movie "Finding Nemo," Dory tries to encourage Marlin to not give up on his son. When Marlin hits rock bottom and he's about to lose hope, Dory encourages him, "Just keep swimming, just keep swimming!" It's not a Bible quote, but it's solid advice.

Three times in this passage, Jesus reminds His disciples to "keep on." As believers, we need to "keep on, keeping on" until we see prayers answered and doors opened. Nothing is over until God says it's over. Don't put qualifiers on your prayers. Just keep praying!

THE AUTHOR OF YOUR STORY

We do this by keeping our eyes on Jesus, the champion who initiates and perfects our faith. Because of the joy awaiting him, he endured the cross, disregarding its shame. Now he is seated in the place of honor beside God's throne.

Hebrews 12:2

In a simple reading of the Bible, you'll discover God never keeps the bad stories out. Some real characters in the Bible did a lot of horrible things, but God still used them. Some of them were murderers, adulterers, liars, cheaters, cowards, and tax collectors, just to name a few. That's not exactly the kinds of things you would want to see on someone's resume.

It's not a book of perfect people, but a book of a perfect God. He loves to redeem people's stories. It gives us hope that nothing is impossible with God. Just because your story did not start well doesn't mean it has to end that way. There's always hope when God is authoring your story.

ISOLATION CAN BE YOUR FRIEND

Early the next morning Jesus went out to an isolated place.
Luke 4:42

We live in a culture where we do not like to be alone. It seems we always must be entertained by our phones or by a device. A lot of people hate being alone or being in silence. Jesus understood the importance of spending alone time with His Father. It was the secret sauce to His ministry.

Isolation is God's invitation for intimacy. If you're feeling isolated, don't waste it. Use it to draw near to God, and he will draw near to you. You'll quickly discover you're not alone because God is with you.

HINDSIGHT IS ALWAYS CLEAR

And we know that God causes everything to work together for the good of those who love God and are called according to his purpose for them.
Romans 8:28

Sometimes God's goodness is best recognized in hindsight. This is a great verse to remind yourself of. Most often, I'm saying it after something has occurred in my life. Nothing that happens in your life escapes God's attention or surprises him. Everything that happens must go through a divine filter before it gets to you.

Just because God allowed something to happen in your life, doesn't mean He liked it. Some things that happen to us are because God understands the outcome will be good for us. The promise we have is that God can use everything we've been through for our good. Nothing gets wasted in God's Kingdom. If He can feed 5,000 men with some fish and chips and send each of the disciples home with a doggie bag, then He's got you covered. He commanded His disciples, "Now gather the leftovers, so that nothing is wasted" (John 6:12). He commands the same thing for your life.

62

WATCH YOUR MOUTH!

Don't use foul or abusive language. Let everything you say be good and helpful, so that your words will be an encouragement to those who hear them.

Ephesians 4:29

Growing up, I would often hear my mother say, "Watch your mouth!" It was usually because I was talking back or saying something I shouldn't. The Apostle James describes the power of the tongue when he says, "But no one can tame the tongue. It is restless and evil, full of deadly poison." James always had a way with words. I suspect he was a blunt person because he didn't mince his words.

As believers, we have an obligation to watch how we use our words. Over the years, I've heard leaders belittle those entrusted to their care. If you feel tall by making someone feel small, you're not a leader; you're a tyrant. Use your words to bring life, not death.

ALL YOU NEED IS A LITTLE FAITH

And it is impossible to please God without faith. Anyone who wants to come to him must believe that God exists and that he rewards those who sincerely seek him.
Hebrews 11:6

Without faith, it is impossible to please God. God never says anything about perfection. The only requirement for pleasing God is faith. That's it. There's nothing we need to add to our salvation. Don't let perfection keep you from doing what God has called you to do.

I would encourage you to read Hebrews 11. This chapter is referred to as the Faith Hall of Fame. They accomplished some great things for God, but none of them were perfect. Their resumes include liars, murderers, adulterers, prostitutes, and cowards. Don't let your fear of perfection keeping you from stepping out in faith in serving God. It doesn't have to be perfect; it just has to be done.

64

DON'T BE SALTY!

Does a fig tree produce olives, or a grapevine produce figs? No, and you can't draw fresh water from a salty spring.
James 3:12

Did you catch the last part of the verse? Go ahead, read it again. It says, "you can't draw fresh water from a salty spring." It's important to remember we are called to have living water flow through our lives as believers. There's nothing wrong with a little bit of salt, but too much of it, and it kills life.

The Dead Sea is an excellent example of this. It is one of the saltiest bodies of water on earth, with almost ten times more salt than ordinary seawater. Aside from algae and some microorganisms, this body of water is entirely devoid of life. There's no seaweed, fish, or any other creatures found in these waters. The moral of the story? Watch your mouth and don't be salty!

WE ALL HAVE TROUBLE

*I have told you all this so that you may have peace in me. Here on earth
you will have many trials and sorrows. But take heart, because I have
overcome the world.*
John 16:33

I hate to break it to you, but trouble is coming. At some point in your life,
you're going to have trouble. When Jesus said these words, He wasn't
preaching doom and gloom. He wasn't having a lack of faith. He was just
being honest. We live in a fallen and sinful world, and we cannot escape
the consequences of sin.

However, the good news is that even though we face trouble, we have
One with us who has overcome all our troubles. God has never lost a
battle; He is still undefeated. Pain is inevitable. Growth is optional. When
we lean into Jesus during our troubles, we can grow from it, and He
promises to use it for our good.

YOU'RE FULL OF IT!

A good person produces good things from the treasury of a good heart,
and an evil person produces evil things from the treasury of an evil
heart. What you say flows from what is in your heart.
Luke 6:45

You can only make a withdrawal from that which you deposit in your life. Over the past few years, we've witnessed countless news media pundits and talking bobble heads say some mean and ridiculous things. When someone calls them on it, they try to excuse their behavior by saying they didn't mean it, or it was an accident. According to this Scripture, the reason the hurtful or vulgar words came out of their mouth is that it was in their heart.

As believers, this should get our attention and make us pause and ask what we are allowing into our spirits. We can't watch certain TV shows or reels on Facebook or Instagram and think they're not going to affect us. You're either consuming healthy things or junk into your heart. It's your choice, but don't be surprised with what comes out when you're squeezed. Choose wisely!

USE A FILTER

Guard your heart above all else, for it determines the course of your life.
Proverbs 4:23

My family and I use a water filtration system at our house because our water tastes terrible. Truthfully, we were pretty sure it was full of impurities as well. When my wife first wanted to purchase a water filtration system, I scoffed because of the price (yes, I can be cheap sometimes). After watching a few videos and reading the research behind them, we concluded it was worth it for our family as it would filter out the unseen impurities in our water.

Likewise, we need to be careful and filter our hearts as well. We should be cautious as to what we give our attention to and what consumes us. Our heart is easily deceived, and we should go to great lengths to guard it against distractions and deception. The only way to guard your heart is through the Word of God and other spiritual disciplines such as prayer, worship, and reflection.

68

GOD PICKED YOU FIRST

*For the L*ORD *delights in his people; he crowns the humble with victory.*
Psalm 149:4

God not only loves you, but He also likes you! As a chubby kid growing up, I was rarely picked first in sports. If God were picking His kickball team today, He would pick you first! How do I know this? Because He's already told us in His Word when He said, "You didn't choose me. I chose you. I appointed you to go and produce lasting fruit, so that the Father will give you whatever you ask for, using my name" (John 15:16). Be blessed and know that God picked you first and He delights in you today!

69

THE RIGHT PERSPECTIVE

*This is the day the L*ORD *has made. We will rejoice and be glad in it.*
Psalm 118:24

Perspective is important. If your name was on the wake-up list today, then you have reason to rejoice. When you believe God is in control of your life, you can confess, "This is the day the Lord has made. We will rejoice and be glad in it" (Psalm 118:24).

70

WELL DONE!

"The master said, 'Well done, my good and faithful servant. You have been faithful in handling this small amount, so now I will give you many more responsibilities. Let's celebrate together!'"
Matthew 25:23

When you get to heaven, the Lord is not going to say, "Well said." He's going to say, "Well done!" The difference between doers and talkers is action. Nothing in your life is going to be a perfect situation. There's always going to be some risk involved or a step of faith involved. You wouldn't need God if there were no risks in life. At some point, you must quit talking, put your boots on, and go serve.

71

DON'T BE MISQUOTED

Those who control their tongue will have a long life; opening your mouth can ruin everything.
Proverbs 13:3

The most difficult person I deal with every day is the guy I shave with. I am my own worst enemy. My mouth is what causes most of my problems, especially with my wife and children. I'm learning to do a better job of controlling my tongue.

To talk less is to get in trouble less. I'm also learning you can't be misquoted for what you don't say. Control your tongue; control your life.

FIGHT FOR YOUR PROMISE

*So the L*ORD *gave to Israel all the land he had sworn to give their ancestors, and they took possession of it and settled there. And the L*ORD *gave them rest on every side, just as he had solemnly promised their ancestors. None of their enemies could stand against them, for the L*ORD *helped them conquer all their enemies. Not a single one of all the good promises the L*ORD *had given to the family of Israel was left unfulfilled; everything he had spoken came true.*
Joshua 21:43-45

Don't be surprised when the enemy is fighting against what the Lord has promised you. Even though the Israelites were given the Promised Land, they still had to fight for it. Some of God's promises in your life are going to require a fight.

The enemy knows he's going to lose, but he's not going to go down without a fight. The good news is that there's more with you than with him. You're in the majority when God is with you. Keep fighting!

PRAISE YOUR WAY THROUGH

After the death of Joshua, the Israelites asked the Lord, *"Which tribe should go first to attack the Canaanites?"*
Judges 1:1-2

After Joshua died, the Israelites still faced unconquered territory. They still had more land to conquer and more ground to overtake. After Moses' death, the Israelites asked the Lord who should lead the way to the battle. The Lord's response was an interesting one. He did not name an individual but a whole tribe. He said Judah was to lead the way into battle. In Hebrew, the word Judah means "to praise." In essence, He was saying praise precedes the battle.

Are you facing a battle in your life? If so, take the time to worship and praise the Lord and see what He will do. Scripture says, "Yet you are holy, enthroned on the praises of Israel" (Psalm 22:3). If that's the case, when you're worshiping the Lord, you're inviting Him into your mess. He can take your mess and make it into a miracle! Take a moment and lift your hands and praise Him for the good things He's done in your life and the good things He's going to do! Go ahead, take a praise break!

UNDERSTANDING THE SEASON THAT YOU'RE IN

So Pharaoh sent for Joseph, and he was quickly brought from the dungeon.
When he had shaved and changed his clothes, he came before Pharaoh.

Genesis 41:14

Joseph was wise enough to understand that he needed to make changes before rushing into Pharaoh's court. Joseph had spent the last several years as a servant in Potiphar's house and as a prisoner in Pharaoh's prison. You can imagine that he looked and dressed like a prisoner while he was in the prison. When he had the opportunity to go before the most powerful leader in the known world, he had to shave and change his clothes. He understood that if he wanted the King to take him seriously, he had to look serious. He also understood that Egyptians preferred clean-shaven people.

I spent several years working in corporate America. My position required a distinct look of a professional. I quickly understood that to be taken seriously by my leadership and clients, I needed to maintain a certain level of decorum. After several years of the corporate world, I transitioned into working with college-age ministry students. It required a different style of dress with them. In both cases, I understood the need to recognize the season in which I served.

What was appropriate for one season of your life may not be appropriate in the next season. It takes discernment as a leader to know what is acceptable in the new season.

A SLING AND A STONE

So David triumphed over the Philistine with only a sling and a stone, for he had no sword.
1 Samuel 17:50

God made the stone; man made the sling. David understood the power of partnering with the Lord. David would do what only he could do, and God would do what only He could do. David had five stones, but he killed Goliath on the first shot. David wasn't lucky; he was prepared. David practiced that shot thousands of times when no one was looking.

Just because you're anointed, doesn't mean you don't have to practice. God anoints prepared people. What you do in private prepares you for what you'll do in public.

ON THE GO MIRACLES

When he saw them, he said, "Go, show yourselves to the priests." And as they went, they were cleansed.
Luke 17:14

This is an interesting story of a miracle. It was unusual because it didn't happen until the lepers put their faith into action. Most of us want to see the miracle, and then we'll get moving. This time Jesus told them to go, and then it would happen. It says, "And as they went, they were cleansed."

There are times in our lives when the Lord is waiting on us to move, and then He'll meet us as we go. Where do you need to step out in faith? Is the Lord waiting on you to take the first step? If you're waiting for the Lord to remove all the risks, then you're going to be waiting a long time. Miracles require risks.

IT'S OKAY TO TALK TO YOURSELF

She said to herself, "If I only touch his cloak, I will be healed."
Matthew 9:21

Your self-talk matters! It could determine your next miracle. In this story, the woman had been bleeding for twelve years. Truthfully, she had spent all she had and was out of options. When you're out of options, it's essential to stay positive. This woman had convinced herself that if she could just touch Jesus, He could heal her.

Her thoughts led to her actions, and her actions led to her miracle. One right thought about Jesus can change your life. Don't let your emotions and past experiences determine what you believe about Jesus' capability. Pay attention to what you say to yourself. Your thoughts matter!

HUMBLE BEGINNINGS

Your beginnings will seem humble, so prosperous will your future be.
Job 8:7

Don't be afraid to start something new or to look like a beginner. Many people never attempt something great because they're afraid to look like a novice or afraid to look foolish. Some of the most remarkable and most significant companies in the world have had humble beginnings. Several companies started in a garage, including Disney, Hewlett-Packard, Amazon, Microsoft, Dell, Virgin, Google, Mattel, MagLite, Yankee Candle Company, and Harley-Davidson. Dave Ramsey started his multimillion-dollar company on a card table in his living room, and this was after he declared bankruptcy. Don't be too afraid to start small!

SAY IT LIKE YOU MEAN IT!

Yet I am confident I will see the Lord's goodness while I am here in the land of the living.
Psalm 27:13

Most scholars believe King David wrote this psalm at one of the lowest points of his life. He wrote it before he became king. During this season, he was running from Saul and was possibly suffering from depression.

I've often quoted this psalm during fearful or difficult times in my life. I will often repeat this verse to myself to build my faith and to remind myself of the promises of God. If God can do it for David, He can do it for you. God is not a respecter of persons. He does respect and keep His word. That's why I always pray the Scriptures because I know God always keeps His word and His word prospers everywhere it is sent (Isaiah 55:11). Pray it, and say it like you mean it!

80

PRAY IT AGAIN!

Then Jesus left them again and prayed the same prayer as before.
Mark 14:39

Sometimes we have to keep praying until our will is aligned with His will. Other times, we must keep praying because some answers just take time. Praying the same prayer is not a lack of faith; it's a matter of persistence.

What prayer have you given up on? Don't beat yourself up. Pray it again!

HE SITS OVER THE FLOOD

*The L*ORD* rules over the floodwaters. The L*ORD* reigns as king forever.*
Psalm 29:10

Faith does not deny your reality. When you have faith for something, it's simply an acknowledgment that you serve a God who is above your circumstances. In the past few weeks, I've been saying to myself, "I'm walking in the midst of a miracle." It's a daily faith declaration that I've adopted for this season. I'm going to keep walking regardless of the flood I'm facing and the negative circumstances. I'm also going to trust that God is in control. Keep on, keeping on!

THE BEST THINGS TAKE TIME

*The foundation of the LORD's Temple was laid in midspring, in the
month of Ziv, during the fourth year of Solomon's reign. The entire
building was completed in every detail by midautumn, in the month of
Bul, during the eleventh year of his reign. So it took seven years to build
the Temple.*
1 Kings 6:37-38

It took seven years to build the temple. Building anything of significance
in your life takes time. There are no shortcuts. Strings must be tightened,
lawns mowed, calls made, emails sent, sermons prepped, prayers prayed,
chords played, pages typed, bats swung, weights lifted, and miles jogged.
If it's worth having, it's worth the time. The best things take time.

IT'S KIND OF A BIG DEAL

*As soon as Jesus heard the news, he left in a boat to a remote area to be
alone. But the crowds heard where he was headed and followed on foot
from many towns.*
Matthew 14:13

Prayer was a big deal to Jesus. Think about it. He never taught His disciples how to preach, but He did teach them how to pray. Prayer was so important that He intentionally took time away from His schedule to pray. He was too busy not to pray. Scripture says that Jesus often withdrew to isolated places to pray (Matt. 14:13; 14:23; Mark 1:35, 45; 3:7, 13; 6:31-32, 46; 9:2; 14:32; Luke 5:16; 6:12-13; 9:18; 11:1; 22:39).

Prayer was His secret sauce. The more ministry He did, the more He prayed. If Jesus was too busy not to pray, then we have some work to do. If you're not sure where to start, start by praying the Lord's Prayer (Matt. 6:9-13; Luke 11:2-4).

YOU'RE NEVER TOO OLD

So Abram departed as the Lord had instructed, and Lot went with him. Abram was seventy-five years old when he left Haran.
Genesis 12:4

Don't ever think you're too old to try something new or make a difference in your family. Abraham was seventy-five years old when he set out from Haran to the Promised Land. This one decision changed his family tree.

I work with college students on a regular basis, and occasionally one of them will joke that I'm getting old. I like to remind them that I'm not old; I just have more experience than they do! Don't let your age keep you from believing you have nothing left to give or contribute to society. Elisha had Elijah, David had Samuel, Joshua had Moses, Paul had Barnabas, and the list could go on. You are needed. Someone needs your gifts and your experience.

MISSION POSSIBLE

For the word of God will never fail.
Luke 1:37

My family and I were at home one day, and my two youngest children were looking at Lego sets online. They came across a fire station set and told my wife and me about it. I had reasoned that if it was $30 or so, we could surprise them with it. I underestimated the price terribly. When I looked up the price, it was $300! I quickly told them we did not have the money to buy an expensive Lego set. Like any self-respecting dad, I told them they needed to pray about it, so we did.

About a week later, a friend texted my wife and said they were moving and had some children's clothes and a few old toys to give us. Their son had outgrown them, so they wanted to bless another family with them. When we came home, a box was on our porch. Upon opening it, it included several good outfits and toys as well. More specifically, it included the exact Lego set my kids had prayed for—and every piece was there. To say I was shocked would be an understatement.

God can treat the little things like big things if we give Him the opportunity. Pray about everything. The least that could happen is nothing. The most that could happen is anything!

THE LORD'S SILENCE

So although Jesus loved Martha, Mary, and Lazarus, he stayed where he was
for the next two days.
John 11:5-6

In this passage, Lazarus was sick, and his sisters sent a message to Jesus to let Him know how bad it was. Lazarus wasn't going to make it if Jesus didn't come and do something. Jesus loved them, but He still delayed in answering their prayer. In fact, He didn't respond at all. He simply stayed where He was for two more days.

Don't mistake the Lord's silence for a lack of concern. He could just be working behind the scenes on your behalf. They were praying for healing; Jesus was waiting for a resurrection. If God is not answering your prayer, it could be that He has bigger plans for your situation than you can see.

THE PERFECT GUIDE

Your word is a lamp to guide my feet and a light for my path.
Psalm 119:105

The Word of God is a flashlight, not a spotlight. Some people won't move until they see the whole picture or have all the details. That is usually not how God operates. He encourages us to "live by believing and not by seeing" (2 Cor. 5:7).

If you're unsure what to do, then do what's in front of you. After that, do the next right thing. Clarity comes with movement. The more you begin to move toward your purpose, the more things become clear to you. As you progress, start to lean into the Word of God for your direction.

88

IT'S GOING TO WORK OUT

And we know that God causes everything to work together for the good of those who love God and are called according to his purpose for them.
Romans 8:28

When you're a follower of Jesus, you can believe His promise that He can turn what was meant to harm you into something that benefits you. There are moments in your life where you can't see how God can use something for your good. During these moments, all you can do is pray and trust. I will often remind myself of this Scripture. I also take the time to remember what God has done in my past to give me hope for my future.

When David was about to face the giant, he remembered the times the Lord delivered him from the lion and the bear (1 Sam. 17:34-36). Your past victories give you hope for your present struggles. There's a reason the word "remember" is used 253 times in Scripture. As humans, we forget things quickly and must be reminded of God's goodness. Remember, rehearse your victories, not your struggles.

THE ONLY WAY THROUGH IS THROUGH

Then Moses raised his hand over the sea, and the L*ORD* *opened up a path through the water with a strong east wind. The wind blew all that night, turning the seabed into dry land. So the people of Israel walked through the middle of the sea on dry ground, with walls of water on each side!*
Exodus 14:21-22

This is a great story of how God delivered the Israelites. Reading it in hindsight, this is a feel-good story of God's deliverance. However, at the moment, the Israelites were scared to death with their backs against the wall. They were stuck with Egypt on one side and the Promised Land on the other side. The only way through was through the sea.

Crossing the Red Sea is a good reminder that transitions can be difficult. Transitions are the hallways of your life. They help you go between the now and the not yet. It's the space between the old and the new. If you're going through a transition, it's essential to stay the course. Don't get scared and turn back.

Where you're going is better than what you had. God has prepared a Promised Land for you!

GRATITUDE IS GOOD MEDICINE

*Let all that I am praise the L*ORD*; with my whole heart, I will praise his holy name. Let all that I am praise the L*ORD*; may I never forget the good things he does for me.*
Psalm 103:1-2

In this psalm, David expressed gratitude because he took the time to recount what the Lord had done in his life. He took the time to list them out in the following few verses. It would be good for you to read the rest of this psalm to see what he wrote. This is one reason I keep a journal. It's a record of my conversations with God, and it enables me to write down what the Lord has done in my life. When times get difficult, I will often go back and encourage myself by reading some of these.

Gratitude and thankfulness are good for the soul. Being thankful is hard, especially when life is not going as we had planned. You could be facing a divorce, financial hardship, or a medical complication, but during these times, you can take the time to not forget what God has done in the past.

SEASONS OF CHANGE

For everything there is a season, a time for every activity under heaven.
Ecclesiastes 3:1

Solomon was known as the wisest man on earth, and he wrote the book of Ecclesiastes. If he was the wisest man on earth, we should probably listen to him and learn a few things. Solomon understood a thing or two about seasons. He spent years preparing and building the temple, and he spent years building and expanding his kingdom. He saw and experienced a lot during his lifetime.

He understood that seasons are not permanent. By their very nature, they're temporary. All of us experience good seasons as well as difficult seasons. Unfortunately, we usually do not get to pick and choose. Winter is coming whether we like it or not. During the cold and harsh seasons, we must remind ourselves that they are only temporary. Don't mistake a short season for a life sentence. Stick to your vision and play the long game. Spring is coming!

IT MATTERS WHERE YOU'RE PLANTED

"But blessed are those who trust in the Lord and have made the Lord their hope and confidence. They are like trees planted along a riverbank, with roots that reach deep into the water. Such trees are not bothered by the heat or worried by long months of drought. Their leaves stay green, and they never stop producing fruit."
Jeremiah 17:7-8

When facing seasons of drought, it matters where you're planted. You need to plant yourself next to the river where the water is flowing. The tough seasons of life require you to send your roots down deeper in God. When you do this, the Lord promises to keep your life fresh and in a continual harvest of fruit. Don't let a season of drought cause you to shrivel up. May it cause you to go deeper in Him!

STRUGGLE ON!

I don't mean to say that I have already achieved these things or that I have already reached perfection. But I press on to possess that perfection for which Christ Jesus first possessed me. No, dear brothers and sisters, I have not achieved it, but I focus on this one thing: Forgetting the past and looking forward to what lies ahead, I press on to reach the end of the race and receive the heavenly prize for which God, through Christ Jesus, is calling us.
Philippians 3:12-14

The Christian life is marked with struggles. Many Christians have bought into the lie that if they're struggling, they're failing. This implies that if they just had a little more faith, things might be different. Paul wrote the book of Philippians while he was in prison. Indeed, he understood some things about struggles.

You need to reframe how you look at struggles. In these verses, Paul encourages fellow believers, "Forgetting the past and looking forward to what lies ahead, I press on to reach the end of the race." I'm not sure about you, but pressing on sounds a lot like struggling to me. Struggles are a sign of progress, not failure. You wouldn't be struggling if you weren't making progress. Struggle on!

KEEP FACING IT

So let's not get tired of doing what is good. At just the right time we will reap a harvest of blessing if we don't give up.
Galatians 6:9

The hardest part of doing anything for God is surviving the messy middle. We can often start something because of excitement and passion, but too many of us get the wind knocked out of us in the middle of it all. Life is a marathon, not a sprint.

Over the years, I've had the privilege of training many students for full-time ministry. Some have done well, and some have not. The most interesting part about those who have done well is that it had nothing to do with their gifts or talents. It had everything to do with perseverance. All of them were willing to persevere and push through the difficult times. They were willing to face it until they made it. If you stay at something long enough, you'll reap the reward. Remember, face it until you make it.

DISCIPLINE IS YOUR FRIEND

No discipline seems pleasant at the time, but painful. Later on, however, it produces a harvest of righteousness and peace for those who have been trained by it.

Hebrews 12:11

The road between what you have and what you want is paved with discipline. Against contrary belief, there are no shortcuts or life hacks for discipline. You must put in the work.

A few years ago, my health was out of control. I was fifty pounds overweight, stressed, winded, and on blood pressure medicine. I knew something had to change, so I started walking in my neighborhood three nights a week. Slowly I started changing my eating habits as well and peppering my life with small disciplines. After six months, I joined a gym and started going four days a week. After several months, I started going six nights a week. It's taken me a few years, but I'm thankful to say I have lost fifty pounds and am now off blood pressure medicine. It wasn't an easy journey, and I'm still learning to instill better discipline and eating habits in my life. Today's discipline becomes tomorrow's habits. Your habits become your life. If I can do it, you can do it!

TALK IS CHEAP

Dear children, let us not love with words or speech but with actions and in truth.
1 John 3:18

Talk is cheap. Words cost you nothing. The Apostle John reminds us that sometimes love has to put boots on. We must walk out love with our actions.

This is also a good reminder that people observe your actions before they'll listen to your words. In our culture, you must earn the right to be heard and speak into someone's life. People will not always remember everything you said, but they will remember how you made them feel. Love requires action, so put your boots on and walk it out.

WORKING FOR GOD

Work willingly at whatever you do, as though you were working for the Lord rather than for people.
Colossians 3:23

What if we approached our jobs as an opportunity to serve the Lord rather than just earning a paycheck? What if we understood that God was our CEO and was watching over us? How would that change our perspective and how we worked? I suspect it would change everything.

The Apostle Paul understood that work becomes worship when we invite God into the process. Don't work another day for just a paycheck; work for the glory of God and see what He does. Worship is not just something we do on Sundays; it's what we do the rest of the week, too. Work is worship.

YOU BELONG HERE

*You made all the delicate, inner parts of my body and knit me together in my
mother's womb. Thank you for making me so wonderfully complex! Your
workmanship is marvelous—how well I know it.*
Psalm 139:13-14

God saw you in the womb and thought you were marvelous. He made
you and designed every part of your life, including your eyes, hair color,
skin color, and temperament. He made you as an expression of His love.
He loved you before you loved Him.

The local gym I belong to is Planet Fitness. Their slogan is, "You
belong here!" I love that because they understand the power of belonging
and the need to make everyone feel welcome. If the Lord brought you
here, you belong here. The Lord loved you long before anyone had an
opinion of you. Don't let the opinion of others keep you from your
destiny.

SKIPPED OVER BUT NOT FORGOTTEN

Then Samuel asked, "Are these all the sons you have?" "There is still the youngest," Jesse replied. "But he's out in the fields watching the sheep and goats." "Send for him at once," Samuel said. "We will not sit down to eat until he arrives."
1 Samuel 16:11

Don't worry if you feel overlooked or passed over. You're in good company. King David was an 8th round draft pick. When Samuel came to Jesse's house to anoint one of his sons to be the next king of Israel, all of Jesse's sons were paraded in front of Samuel. The problem was that God had not chosen any of them to be king. After the parade was over, Samuel looked at Jesse and asked if he had any more sons. There was the one son who was watching the sheep. He was the runt of the litter and he had been forgotten. Truthfully, his father didn't view him as king material, so he didn't invite him to the show.

It's not the size of the man that counts. It's the size of his heart. David was a man after God's own heart. Man might skip over you, but God has not forgotten, and He keeps good records. Keep serving faithfully, and your time will come.

100

DON'T BE SHAKEN

"For the mountains may move and the hills disappear, but even then my
faithful love for you will remain. My covenant of blessing will never be broken,"
says the LORD, *who has mercy on you.*
Isaiah 54:10

Earthquakes have a way of shaking things up. What's not grounded with a firm foundation gets knocked over and shaken down. At some point, we are all going to experience a personal earthquake. These moments in life take us by surprise and come out of nowhere. When this happens, we must make sure we are planted on a firm foundation and rooted in God's Word.

Things are being shaken right now, but God's covenant promises remain immovable. Hang on to His Word during this season and know God's love for you can never be shaken.

FLIPPING TABLES

Jesus entered the temple courts and drove out all who were buying and selling there. He overturned the tables of the money changers and the benches of those selling doves. "It is written," he said to them, "'My house will be called a house of prayer,' but you are making it 'a den of robbers.'"
Matthew 21:11-12

Most portraits of Jesus picture Him as weak, meek, and mild. For some reason, we have reduced Christianity to just being nice. However, when you read the Gospels, you get a different picture of Jesus. He was nice, but He was also bold. He was good to sinners, but He was rough on Pharisees. It seems like religious people who don't love sinners get on His nerves.

In this Scripture, the religious people had turned the Temple into a marketplace. By outward appearances, things were prospering in the Temple, but Jesus saw past their hypocrisy, and it infuriated Him. He couldn't just stand around and continue to let the desecration go on. To everyone's surprise, He came in a blaze of glory and turned everything upside down. Some days Jesus withdrew to pray. Some days He flipped tables. As a leader, it's essential to know which one is needed.

SERVING WHEN IT'S HARD

Meanwhile, the boy Samuel served the Lord *by assisting Eli. Now in those days, messages from the* Lord *were very rare, and visions were quite uncommon. One night Eli, who was almost blind by now, had gone to bed.*

1 Samuel 3:1-2

Samuel grew up serving at the tabernacle. He grew up serving Eli, and unfortunately, Eli had lost his vision (spiritually and literally). Samuel also grew up watching the bad examples of Eli's two sons. They were scoundrels, to say the least. They would regularly steal the best meat from the sacrifices and sleep with women as they came to worship at the tabernacle. They were hardly role models for an impressionable young boy. Despite all of this, Samuel kept a good attitude towards Eli. He seemed to instinctively know it was not his place to discipline Eli or his sons. It was his job to serve.

There will be times in your life when you are placed under difficult leadership. During these times, you have to decide how to respond. Good or bad, you serve through leadership, not around it. In the end, God blessed Samuel, and he would serve as the greatest prophet in the Old Testament.

THE VALUE OF A MENTOR

When they came to the other side, Elijah said to Elisha, "Tell me what I can do
for you before I am taken away." And Elisha replied, "Please let me inherit a
double share of your spirit and become your successor."
2 Kings 2:9

Elisha would eventually be the successor of Elijah. At his request, God gave him a double portion of Elijah's anointing, and he would go on to do twice as many miracles as Elijah. Elisha was able to go twice as far in life because he had a good mentor. A good mentor will help you to go further and faster. The best mentors are already successful and busy, but they're worth the effort to pursue.

Some of my best mentors have been in person, and some have been from a distance. The best mentors have written books that you can buy on Amazon, and you can read about what they've been able to accomplish. For $20 or less, you can learn in a few hours what they learned in a lifetime. It's a small price to pay for someone else's experience. If you want to be an Elisha, you need an Elijah in your life.

CHANGE YOUR THINKING, CHANGE YOUR FUTURE

What's more, I am changing your name. It will no longer be Abram. Instead, you will be called Abraham, for you will be the father of many nations.
Genesis 17:5

At the age of ninety-nine, God changed Abram's name. Abraham's new name would mean "father of many nations." The irony is that God changed his name while he was still childless. Abraham walked around a year speaking and hearing his new name before he received the promise of Isaac at the age of 100 (Gen. 21:5). The Lord had to change his thinking before he could give him the promise. Abraham became what he believed. What promises do you need to start proclaiming over your life?

GOD HAS BEEN THINKING ABOUT YOU

*Even before he made the world, God loved us and chose us in Christ to
be holy and without fault in his eyes.*
Ephesians 1:4

Have you ever received a robocall on your phone from someone trying to
reach you about your extended car warranty? It's almost comical now. On
the same note, Jesus chose you long before you chose Him. Before God
made you, you were on His mind! He loved you before you were born,
and He chose to bring you life. You are the apple of His eye and the object
of His affection. Even when you feel unloved and unworthy, you need to
know God loves you. He loved you long before you were born, and He
will love you long afterwards.

DEAL WITH YOUR PRIVATE LIFE

When King David heard what had happened, he was very angry.
2 Samuel 13:21

This chapter and subsequent chapters tell the story of David and Absalom. It's a story of bitterness, anger, resentment, betrayal, and death. It all started when Absalom's beautiful sister, Tamar, was raped by her half-brother Amnon. The Scripture records that when King David heard about it, he was very angry. This was an underestimate. David should have been furious, but the problem is that he did nothing about it. There is no record of David disciplining his rogue sin or confronting the sin in his son's life. When he didn't deal with Amnon's sin, it resulted in overwhelming bitterness in the heart of Absalom. Absalom's bitterness resulted in the murder of Amnon, his brother. It almost cost David his throne and his life. In the end, Absalom died a bitter and resentful man. David could have avoided all of this by dealing with the sins in his private life. He was a warrior on the battlefield but a coward at home.

What you fail to confront in your private life could eventually destroy your public life. It's better to deal with problems privately, so they don't spill over publicly. It's better to deal with sin in private, so it isn't exposed in public.

DON'T LOSE YOUR VISION

*So the Philistines captured him and gouged out his eyes. They took him
to Gaza, where he was bound with bronze chains and forced to grind
grain in the prison.*
Judges 16:21

Samson was the poster child of judges in the Old Testament. He was the
total package consisting of good looks, muscles, charm, wit, and anointing. By outward appearances, he had it all. Despite having all the right
characteristics, he still lacked character. His arrogance and lack of character would ultimately lead to his downfall. For so long, he flirted with
the Philistines (sin) and got by with it. He bought into the lie that if he can
get by with it once, he can get by with it again. He mistook God's silence
as permission. Sometimes God is silent because He's giving you the grace
to repent. Samson never learned this, and eventually, the Philistines
captured him and gouged out his eyes.

Life Lesson from Samson: Samson lost his vision long before he lost
his sight.

FIND THE OPPORTUNITY OR THE OPPOSITION

The LORD now said to Moses, "Send out men to explore the land of Canaan, the land I am giving to the Israelites. Send one leader from each of the twelve ancestral tribes." So Moses did as the LORD commanded him. He sent out twelve men, all tribal leaders of Israel, from their camp in the wilderness of Paran.
Numbers 13:1-3

Moses sent out twelve spies to spy out the Promised Land. Joshua and Caleb were the only two that received an inheritance (Joshua 15). When they came back to give their report, they never denied their reality. They chose to focus on the opportunity, not the opposition.

We always have the option to determine what we focus on. Some God-given opportunities come in the form of resistance. You must push past the resistance to find the opportunity. Faith and prayer are the vehicles that will take you there. Keep praying and believing!

YOUR SEED WILL MEET YOUR NEED

When Isaac planted his crops that year, he harvested a hundred times more grain than he planted, for the LORD blessed him.
Genesis 26:12

Isaac was living in a severe drought. Initially, he decided to go down to Gerar, which was Philistine territory. Even during a drought, the Lord blessed him. During a drought, the natural response of most people is to hoard and withhold their seed. Instead, Isaac chose to sow seed for his need and reaped a hundred-fold harvest. While everyone else was scrounging, Isaac was reaping.

Don't let the conditions around you keep you from sowing. Never underestimate the potential of your seed. Isaac sowed during a famine and reaped one hundred-fold.

110

BE ANXIOUS FOR NOTHING

Don't worry about anything; instead, pray about everything. Tell God what you need, and thank him for all he has done. Then you will experience God's peace, which exceeds anything we can understand. His peace will guard your hearts and minds as you live in Christ Jesus.
Philippians 4:6-7

This morning I found myself being anxious. As I was in my kitchen, the Holy Spirit reminded me of Philippians 4:6-7. Truthfully, I could not remember the whole verse. I had to go and look it up. As I read it, the Holy Spirit whispered, "You have to give me something to work with. I can't remind you of what you don't know."

I have committed myself to memorizing this verse, and I will be intentional about memorizing other Scriptures. The best time to memorize the Word is before you need it. The second best time to memorize it is now. I would encourage you to ask the Holy Spirit to help you memorize His Word during this season, as it will be what sustains your faith during difficult times in the future.

111

UNDER YOUR FEET

You will trample upon lions and cobras; you will crush fierce lions and serpents
under your feet!
Psalm 91:13

Scripture is clear that we will face threats from our adversaries, but we will trample them under our feet. As believers, we are called to walk over whatever tries to keep us under. This means we cannot lie down and give up. When you lie down and give up, the enemy is the one trampling you. Get back up and keep walking through your trial. Your faith will be rewarded.

112

LYING DOWN

He lets me rest in green meadows; he leads me beside peaceful streams.
Psalm 23:2

As children, most of us were made to lie down at a specific time every night. We didn't like bedtimes, and we usually found any excuse to get up. We wanted to be in control, and we didn't want to be told what to do. Truthfully, we still feel this way even though we are older.

At certain times of your life, God will make you lie down and be still. Frankly, it's uncomfortable, and we feel out of control. When you feel out of control, God is in control. The good news: it's a green pasture. It's one that is life-giving and fruitful. Your perspective will determine what you glean from this season.

THE GOOD OLE DAYS WERE NOT THAT GOOD

"The future glory of this Temple will be greater than its past glory, says the LORD *of Heaven's Armies. And in this place I will bring peace. I, the* LORD *of Heaven's Armies, have spoken!"*
Haggai 2:9

Have you ever heard someone say, "I miss the good ole days!" They seem to have a nostalgia for a specific time period of their life. Frankly, I'm glad the good ole days are behind us. I have no desire to go back. God has brought me a long way.

What is ahead of you is better than what is behind you! Keep walking and experience the peace of God in your life. Scripture reminds us that God has kept the best until now (John 2:10)!

114

THE WORD HAS A PURPOSE

The rain and snow come down from the heavens and stay on the ground to water the earth. They cause the grain to grow, producing seed for the farmer and bread for the hungry. It is the same with my word. I send it out, and it always produces fruit. It will accomplish all I want it to, and it will prosper everywhere I send it.
Isaiah 55:10-11

Isaiah compares the Word of God to seed that gets planted. When a seed is planted in good soil, we can expect a harvest. When we speak the Word of God, we are sowing seed in our lives. If our words are seed, we need to be careful what kind of seed we are planting. Proverbs 18:21 declares that the power of life and death are in the tongue.

If you're not sure what to pray, then pray Scripture. Start by praying Psalm 23 and Psalm 91. God declares that His Word cannot fail and it always produces fruit!

115

LITTLE THINGS LEAD TO BIG THINGS

If you are faithful in little things, you will be faithful in large ones. But if you are dishonest in little things, you won't be honest with greater responsibilities.
Luke 16:10

Little things lead to big things. That's how the kingdom operates. Young leaders often want to jump to significant responsibilities, but they often neglect the little things along the way. When they do this, they are missing out on God-given opportunities. When you treat the little things like big things, you'll be qualified for bigger things.

JUST A REMINDER

"Look at the lilies and how they grow. They don't work or make their clothing, yet Solomon in all his glory was not dressed as beautifully as they are. And if God cares so wonderfully for flowers that are here today and thrown into the fire tomorrow, he will certainly care for you. Why do you have so little faith? " And don't be concerned about what to eat and what to drink. Don't worry about such things. These things dominate the thoughts of unbelievers all over the world, but your father already knows your needs. Seek the Kingdom of God above all else, and he will give you everything you need."
Luke 12:27-31

Sometimes we need to be reminded of what we already know. It's not that we don't believe it. It's just that we get busy, and life has a way of knocking us off balance. The reminder is that if we seek God first, He will take care of the rest.

A few weeks ago, I told my wife that I would have to purchase new tires for my car this summer. I didn't want to buy them because other expenses were coming up, but I knew they couldn't wait too much longer. A couple weeks later, a businessman who attends our church and who owns a tire dealership called my office. He said he had a set of tires to give away as a "thank you" from one of his vendors. I was shocked and asked if this was a joke. "No," he replied. "One of my vendors that I sell a lot of tires for is giving me a set to give away to someone who needs them, so I called the church office and here we are!" I couldn't believe this. Only God knew that I needed a new set of tires. Apparently, that's all that mattered. A few hours later, I was driving around with a new set of tires. When you seek God first, He takes care of the rest!

117

PRAY THE PROMISES, NOT THE PROBLEMS

This I declare about the Lord: *He alone is my refuge, my place of safety; he is my God, and I trust him. For he will rescue you from every trap and protect you from deadly disease. He will cover you with his feathers. He will shelter you with his wings. His faithful promises are your armor and protection.*
Psalm 91:2-4

When facing fear, you pray the promises, not the problems. What you feed grows and what you starve dies. The best way to destroy fear is to starve it to death. The only way to do this is to replace your fears with the promises of God.

I regularly speak several Scriptures over my life. I do this because I constantly have to slay fear in my life. Fear left unattended is like a vine that grows wildly in your life and threatens to choke the life out of your faith. Don't play nice with fear. Kill it!

118

ABOVE THE NOISE OF THE CROWD

Then a mighty roar rose from the crowd, and with one voice they shouted, "Kill him, and release Barabbas to us!" (Barabbas was in prison for taking part in an insurrection in Jerusalem against the government, and for murder.)
Luke 23:18-19

We live in a social media-driven world where many people want a big following and want to be an influencer. It's easy to look at someone and believe they know what's best just because they call themselves a leader or an influencer. Just because someone is loud and has a big platform doesn't mean you should listen to them. The crowd shouted for Barabbas when they should have been asking for Jesus.

GET THE BIBLE THROUGH YOU

*Don't copy the behavior and customs of this world, but let God
transform you into a new person by changing the way you think. Then
you will learn to know God's will for you, which is good and pleasing
and perfect.*
Romans 12:2

God isn't as concerned about you getting through the Bible as He is about it getting through you. The only way to change the way you think is to renew your mind with the Word of God. Unfortunately, before you belonged to the Kingdom of the Light, you were in darkness, and you believed the enemy's lies. The only way to rid yourself of the lies you once believed is to know the truth. When you know the truth, it sets you free (John 8:32).

When you take the time to read the Word, it will transform and renew your mind. Thankfully, I do not think the way I used to, and I am not the person I used to be. I'm not perfect, but I am making progress!

120

PROPHETIC DECLARATIONS

But if you refuse to serve the LORD, then choose today whom you will serve. Would you prefer the gods your ancestors served beyond the Euphrates? Or will it be the gods of the Amorites in whose land you now live? But as for me and my family, we will serve the LORD."
Joshua 24:15

Joshua made this statement to the Israelites right before his death. Joshua was making a prophetic declaration over his family. He was about to die and would soon not be in the picture. Even when you're not sure about what's going to happen in the future, you must rely on the promises of God. You can rely on them because you know they cannot fail.

If you have a prodigal child or someone in your family who is not serving the Lord, you can make this your prayer and a prophetic declaration, "But as for me and my family, we will serve the Lord." When you don't know what to pray, pray the promises.

121

PRESS ON!

No, dear brothers and sisters, I have not achieved it, but I focus on this one thing: Forgetting the past and looking forward to what lies ahead, I press on to reach the end of the race and receive the heavenly prize for which God, through Christ Jesus, is calling us.
Philippians 3:13-14

The Apostle Paul knew a thing or two about struggles. He had been beaten multiple times, stoned, left for dead, hungry, naked, jailed on numerous occasions, betrayed, and other things as well. He was a man of struggles. Just because you're struggling, it doesn't mean you're failing. Struggling is proof you haven't given up. Press on today!

BE THE ANSWER TO SOMEONE'S PRAYERS

Then Abraham prayed to God, and God healed Abimelech, his wife, and his female servants, so they could have children. For the LORD had caused all the women to be infertile because of what happened with Abraham's wife, Sarah.
Genesis 20:17-18

God honors those who pray for someone else's miracle while they're waiting for their own miracle. Abraham was able to pray for other people's wombs to be open while his wife's womb remained closed. Abraham learned to pray and trust God for others while he waited for the miracle in his own household.

If you have a need in your life, pray that God will meet that need in someone else's life. If you have a struggling teenager, it might be an opportunity to pray for someone else's teenager who is struggling. If your business is struggling, then pray for someone else's business. Be the answer to someone else's prayers.

123

DREAM BIGGER

Now all glory to God, who is able, through his mighty power at work within us,
to accomplish infinitely more than we might ask or think.
Ephesians 3:20

In Genesis 15, we see an encounter between God and Abraham. Abraham had been praying and asking God for an heir to his household. Truth be told, Abraham thought this was a big deal. God took him outside of his tent and told him to count the stars. The stars would represent Abraham's future offspring. Abraham wanted a son; God wanted a nation. Like Abraham, we need to be delivered from small-mindedness. We serve a God who can do immeasurably more than we can ask, think, or imagine. Go ahead! You now have permission to dream bigger!

ONCE MORE FAITH

*Then he lay down on the child's body, placing his mouth on the child's mouth,
his eyes on the child's eyes, and his hands on the child's hands. And as he
stretched out on him, the child's body began to grow warm again! Elisha got up,
walked back and forth across the room once, and then stretched himself out
again on the child. This time the boy sneezed seven times and opened his eyes!*
2 Kings 4:34-35

As believers, we need a "once more" kind of faith. Some situations
require you to pray once more. Elisha didn't give up the first time he
prayed for a miracle and didn't get the answer. He got up, paced back and
forth in the room, and tried again. Just because you don't see the answer,
it doesn't mean the Lord's not working. Some miracles just need time to
warm up!

125

SPIRITUAL GANGRENE

Look after each other so that none of you fails to receive the grace of God. Watch out that no poisonous root of bitterness grows up to trouble you, corrupting many.
Hebrews 12:15

It is easy to see the effect of bitterness in people's lives. Bitterness is spiritual gangrene and is very contagious. When left untreated, it can quickly spread throughout the body. If left untreated, it has the potential to infect a lot of people quickly.

If you're struggling with bitterness, the only way to treat it is to confess it and repent of it. Don't delay; deal with it today.

GOD'S FORMULA FOR PROVISION

As long as the earth remains, there will be planting and harvest, cold and heat,
summer and winter, day and night.
Genesis 8:22

God's process for provision is a simple formula of seed-time-harvest. God's natural order of creation operates by this law. Every farmer on the planet understands this process, and they use it to supply the needs of their lives. Your need will be met by your seed.

People don't sow because they don't believe God will return a harvest. Trust God's process for your provision. You must sow a seed, wait for the appointed time, and then reap a harvest.

127

YOU HAVE THE ADVANTAGE

*As long as Moses held up the staff in his hand, the Israelites had the
advantage. But whenever he dropped his hand, the Amalekites gained
the advantage.*
Exodus 17:11

In the book of Exodus, the Israelites were fighting the Amalekites. They
were descendants of the Rephidim, which were the giants of the land. In
the natural, they were outmatched, but in the supernatural, the odds
were in their favor. When Moses began to lift his hands toward heaven,
God began to reach His hands down toward the earth. As long as Moses
kept his hands up, the battle leaned in their favor, but the enemy started
to win when his hands went down.

We may not battle physical giants today, but we are in a battle with
unseen forces. Paul writes in Ephesians 6:12, "For we are not fighting
against flesh-and-blood enemies, but against evil rulers and authorities of
the unseen world, against mighty powers in this dark world, and against
evil spirits in the heavenly places." Spiritual battles must be fought with
spiritual weapons. Your worship is your weapon.

As believers, when we lift our hands in worship and in prayer, we
have an advantage over our enemies. Let's not give up our advantage.

STOP WISHING AND START ASKING

If you, then, though you are evil, know how to give good gifts to your children,
how much more will your father in heaven give good gifts to those who ask him!
Matthew 7:11

A while back, while I was sitting at the kitchen table eating a bowl of ice cream, my youngest daughter came up to me and said, "That looks good. I wish I had a bowl of ice cream." I looked at her and said, "Would you like some ice cream?" She responded with a resounding, "Yes!" I looked at her and said, "Sweetheart, you don't have to wish for stuff. All you have to do is ask and if Daddy has it, he will give it to you."

A lot of us approach our Heavenly Father in the same manner. Instead of praying and asking Him for our needs, we simply resort to wishing for it, as if we were a beggar with no hope of our desires being met. We are not beggars. We are children of the King, and His desire is to give good gifts to us. Stop wishing and start praying. God never commanded us to wish; He commanded us to pray. There is power in prayer.

129

BE A DREAMER

His brothers responded, "So you think you will be our king, do you? Do you actually think you will reign over us?" And they hated him all the more because of his dreams and the way he talked about them.

Genesis 37:8

Not everyone in your life is going to celebrate your dreams. In fact, those closest to you will probably mock you for it. The problem is that those closest to you see you as you are now, rather than the person who will become qualified for the dream. On the other hand, God sees you for who you will be tomorrow, not for who you are today.

People who don't dream, despise those who do. Don't share your dreams with just anyone. Make sure they're qualified to hear your dreams.

130

SERVE WHILE YOU WAIT

And they replied, "We both had dreams last night, but no one can tell us what they mean." "Interpreting dreams is God's business," Joseph replied. "Go ahead and tell me your dreams."
Genesis 40:8

When Joseph was 17 years old, he dreamed of one day being in leadership and doing great things for God. It would be several years later before he would see the dream come to pass. In fact, he was 30 years old when the dream became reality. That's a long time to wait. During his time of waiting, he went from the pit to the house, the prison, and to the palace. Along the way, he developed his gifts and used them to help others with their dreams while he waited on his dream to come true.

Joseph could have become bitter about waiting on his dreams while watching others receive blessings and promotions, but he chose to serve while he waited. Serving would eventually be his ticket out of prison. Help someone else with their dream while you wait for yours. Eventually, someone will need your gifts.

131

THE MAJORITY RULES

"Don't be afraid!" Elisha told him. "For there are more on our side than
on theirs!"
2 Kings 6:16

Elisha and his servant found themselves trapped in a city surrounded by
a great army of chariots and horses. In the natural, they were surrounded
and outnumbered, but Elisha didn't operate in the natural realm. He
chose to live supernaturally through the eyes of faith. What he saw in the
spirit was greater than what was in the natural.

When we are overwhelmed and feeling surrounded by the enemy, we
must choose to look at the situation through the eyes of faith. I often
quote this verse and remind myself of a simple formula: You + God =
Majority.

132

IT'S IN GOD'S HANDS

But I am trusting you, O Lord, saying, "You are my God!" My future is in your hands. Rescue me from those who hunt me down relentlessly.
Psalm 31:14-15

Many years ago, I was facing uncertainty in the position I held. Truthfully, I was afraid that my boss was going fire me. It was a season of doing the best I could, but it felt like I was coming up short. In a moment of desperation, I turned to the Lord in prayer and fasting. In response, the Lord showed me this verse, which became a source of strength for me.

I began to trust that my life and my future were in the hands of God, not a person, not a business, and not an organization. God alone was my source. If you are facing a situation today and are fearful about your future, take time to make this verse a declaration.

The psalmist actually took the time to say it. Notice that the verse says, "But I am trusting you; O Lord, saying...." So, go ahead. Say it!

133

RUN YOUR OWN RACE

Therefore, since we are surrounded by such a huge crowd of witnesses to the life of faith, let us strip off every weight that slows us down, especially the sin that so easily trips us up. And let us run with endurance the race God has set before us.
Hebrews 12:1

The writer of Hebrews encourages the believers to run with perseverance and to run the race marked out for them. In a race, every runner has a lane marked out for them. To not be disqualified from the race, they must stay in their lane and run their own race. If they drift over into someone else's lane, someone can get hurt, and they'll be disqualified from the race.

It's essential to run your own race and not focus on what other people are doing around you. We often get out of our lanes because of jealousy or because of distractions. In either case, they can both lead to being disqualified. When you understand your calling and gifts, you won't drift off into other lanes because you'll be too focused on running your own race. Athletes run in the direction of their focus. Focus on Jesus, and you'll finish the race.

BUILD IT AND THEY WILL COME

Pairs of all creatures that have the breath of life in them came to Noah and entered the ark.
Genesis 7:15

Noah built the ark, and then the animals came. God brought the provision to Noah only after he was ready to receive it. Maybe we're not seeing what we want to see in our lives because we've not created the room to receive it.

What has the Lord instructed you to do first? Is it sowing, serving, or building something? Provision typically shows up after we've stepped out in faith, not before.

135

GOD WILL MAKE A WAY

They entered the house and saw the child with his mother, Mary, and they bowed down and worshiped him. Then they opened their treasure chests and gave him gifts of gold, frankincense, and myrrh.

Matthew 2:11

The story of the three wise men visiting Jesus was anything but a Hallmark movie. Joseph was awakened in the middle of the night and told to pack their bags and flee because Herod was sending people to search for Jesus so they might kill him. This was hardly a vacation. God was about to send Jesus' family on an all-expense-paid trip to Egypt--except Egyptians didn't like Israelites. It would require Joseph and his family to live as exiles in a foreign land.

The three wise men brought gold, frankincense, and myrrh to Mary and Joseph. It was a prophetic sign of Jesus' life and death, but it was also a gift that would sustain their family as they had to flee to Egypt. Remember, God keeps provision for you, not from you. Even in difficult seasons, God will make a way.

FROM THE HOUSE TO THE PALACE

But Joseph refused. "Look," he told her, "my master trusts me with everything in his entire household. No one here has more authority than I do. He has held back nothing from me except you, because you are his wife. How could I do such a wicked thing? It would be a great sin against God."
Genesis 39:8-9

In this passage, Joseph had been promoted to chief steward over Potiphar's house. Scripture indicates that day after day, Potiphar's wife put pressure on him to sleep with her. Truthfully, Joseph could have used his position to sleep with her, and this would have secured him more favor, and no one would have ever known, except for God. During this trial, Joseph intrinsically knew this was a test and, ultimately, it would be a sin against God. That was enough to motivate him to do right. Little did he know that God had more significant plans for his life than running Potiphar's house!

God was using Potiphar's house to prepare him for Pharaoh's palace. How you act in Potiphar's house will determine how God can trust you in Pharaoh's palace. Don't let the trial of a short season disqualify you from your long-term destiny.

137

GOD HAS A PLAN

For I know the plans I have for you," says the LORD. *"They are plans for good and not for disaster, to give you a future and a hope."*
Jeremiah 29:11

The Lord says you are not an accident. You're not a mistake, and you're not here by chance. Your parents might have given up on you or gave you up for adoption, but God still had a plan for you.

You're here because God planned for you to be here. If He planned for you to be here, then He has an assignment for you. His assignment will give you hope and a future. God's plan is greater than your pain.

138

HE'S LORD OVER ALL

Both day and night belong to you; you made the starlight and the sun.
You set the boundaries of the earth, and you made both summer and
winter.
Psalm 74:16-17

He is Lord over the good and the dark times in your life. He's Lord over the plentiful and the seasons of famine. He's Lord over cancer. He's Lord over bankruptcy. He's Lord over depression. He's Lord over all things.

He sets up boundaries over your life. There's nothing that goes on in your life that is not under His control. He can be trusted even during the darkest days. His plans toward you are good and not to harm you. Trust Him!

BE ABOUT THE KING'S BUSINESS

Then I, Daniel, was overcome and lay sick for several days. Afterward I got up and performed my duties for the king, but I was greatly troubled by the vision and could not understand it.

Daniel 8:27

There are times when circumstances in our lives are beyond our understanding. These times leave us tired and exhausted, and they leave us wondering what we should be doing. You might be asking, "What do I do now?" Daniel reminds us to get up and get about the King's business! There's more to be done. There are more mountains to climb. You have more miracles to see! There are more lost people to be saved and more people to be discipled. When you don't know what to do, do the next right thing.

140

THANK YOU

Give thanks to the Lord, for he is good. His love endures forever. Give thanks to the God of gods. His love endures forever. Give thanks to the Lord of lords: His love endures forever.
Psalm 136:1-3

Have you ever found yourself praying, and you ran out of things to say, or you don't know what to say? Sometimes the best prayer is, "Thank you."

In this passage, the psalmist is so overwhelmed with thankfulness to God that he repeats it three times in the first part of his prayer. He's not babbling; he's stuck on the goodness of God. When was the last time you stopped and just shared with God what you're thankful for? Go ahead, make a gratitude list for Him.

141

YOUR SURE FOUNDATION

In that day he will be your sure foundation, providing a rich store of salvation, wisdom, and knowledge. The fear of the LORD will be your treasure.

Isaiah 33:6

During times of uncertainty, God is our sure and steady foundation. He has all we need stored away for us, including deliverance, wisdom, provision, and knowledge. The key that unlocks this treasure is the fear of the Lord. To fear the Lord is more than just being afraid. It's a strong desire to honor Him and not do anything that would cause separation between you and Him. Holy fear keeps you from sinning.

BE CAREFUL HOW YOU JUDGE OTHERS

*Do not judge others, and you will not be judged. For you will be treated
as you treat others. The standard you use in judging is the standard by
which you will be judged.*
Matthew 7:2

A lot of people are experts on their opinions. They seem to know everything and have a knack for calling out the shortcomings in everyone around them. People like this don't know what they don't know.

How you judge others is how you'll be judged. It never hurts to extend a little grace to someone. You might just need some yourself one day.

DON'T GIVE UP!

Then Jesus took her by the hand and said in a loud voice, "My child,
get up!"
Luke 8:54

Jairus was the leader of a local synagogue, and his only daughter was dying. He was desperate enough to go to Jesus and beg for Him to heal her. The only problem was there was a delay in Jesus getting there. There seemed to be interruptions with other people's problems. While they dealt with the interruptions, a messenger arrived and said it was too late because the girl was dead.

There are moments in life when we're going to find our dream lying there dead. By outward appearances, this situation was too far gone, and nothing else could be done. However, Jesus was no ordinary rabbi. He was the Resurrection and the Life. Death would not have victory in this moment.

Don't give up on your dream. You thought your dream was dead and too far gone. Jesus says to you, "Just have faith," and get up!

144

GOD CAN DO MORE THAN YOU THINK

Now all glory to God, who is able, through his mighty power at work within us,
to accomplish infinitely more than we might ask or think.
Ephesians 3:20

There are approximately 7,500 varieties of apples in the world. If God can create that many different apples, I'm pretty sure He's not lacking in resources or creativity. He made that many apples for no other reason than just because He could.

God's power is at work within us to accomplish more than we can dream. When Abraham asked God for an heir, God took him outside and told him to count the stars. I'm not sure if Abraham tried, but he lost that bet. I've tried counting the stars, and it's impossible. There's always more, and I believe there's always more God wants to do in our lives if we will trust Him.

145

PROBLEMS BENEFIT YOU

We can rejoice, too, when we run into problems and trials, for we know that they help us develop endurance. And endurance develops strength of character, and character strengthens our confident hope of salvation. And this hope will not lead to disappointment. For we know how dearly God loves us because he has given us the Holy Spirit to fill our hearts with his love.
Romans 5:3-5

As an avid gym-goer, I quickly discovered if I wanted to gain more muscle and get in shape, I would have to apply more resistance to my life. As much as it pained me, the resistance did not stop me from growing; it fueled it.

Problems provide benefits to your life. Problems cause you to grow and to develop perseverance and character. Allow the difficulties you encounter to fuel your capacity to grow deep roots and learn to overcome what's thrown at you.

LISTEN TO THE RIGHT VOICES

This is what they reported to Moses: "We went to the land where you sent us. It really is a land flowing with milk and honey. Here's some of its fruit. But the people who live there are strong, and the cities have walls and are very large. We even saw the descendants of Anak there. The Amalekites live in the Negev. The Hittites, Jebusites, and Amorites live in the mountain region. And the Canaanites live along the coast of the Mediterranean Sea and all along the Jordan River."
Numbers 13:27-29

Moses sent out twelve men to spy out the Promised Land. After forty days, they returned with some produce from the land and a report of what they saw. Their report focused more on the giants than the promise. Out of the twelve men who were sent out, ten of them offered a bad report. Only two of the men, Caleb and Joshua, saw the opportunity.

The Israelites did not enter the Promised Land because they listened to the voices of the ten who brought back a bad report. Think about that! Israel lost the battle in their mind before they stepped one foot into the Promised Land. Israel was made to keep wandering the desert for 40 years because ten men couldn't control their thought life. Make sure you're listening to the right voices in your life. Your thoughts matter.

147

THEY WILL FLOURISH LIKE A PALM TREE

*But the godly will flourish like palm trees and grow strong like the
cedars of Lebanon.*
Psalm 92:12

My wife and I went to college in Florida. On weekends we would spend
time studying at the beach. (Okay, we spent more time enjoying the
beach than studying!) One thing I was always amazed at was the flexi-
bility and strength of the palm trees. They are typically found in tropical
climates, where they encounter hurricanes or tropical storms. The palm
tree is a surprisingly strong tree that is not easily broken. They have deep
roots that keep them anchored, so they won't topple over or become
uprooted when they face a storm. Maybe that's what the psalmist meant
when he said the righteous are like palm trees. When you're righteous,
you might be bent, but you won't be broken!

148

QUIT MAKING EXCUSES

The lazy person claims, "There's a lion out there! If I go outside, I might be killed!"
Proverbs 22:13

It's easier to make excuses than it is to make progress. There is never a perfect time to do something. If you're waiting on the perfect time to do something for God, you're going to be waiting a long time. Faith requires risks. We certainly need to use wisdom and the discernment of the Holy Spirit. Still, there will never be a perfect situation in your life. Don't wait for your emotions to feel like doing something. The more I do something, the more I feel like doing it. You'll either find an excuse, or you'll find a way. Quit making excuses and get outside of your comfort zone.

149

TODAY IS THE DAY

This is the day the LORD has made. We will rejoice and be glad in it.
Psalm 118:24

If your name was on the wake-up list this morning, then you have a purpose and something for which to be thankful. You can rejoice knowing God still has a purpose and a plan for your life. Don't discredit yourself because you think you're too old. Moses was 80 years old when God called him to lead Israel into the Promised Land. Caleb was 80 years old when God gave him a mountain to conquer. You're not old; you're just getting started!

150

GOD IS FOR YOU

What shall we say about such wonderful things as these? If God is for us, who can ever be against us?
Romans 8:31

Contrary to the common beliefs and lies of the enemy, God is for you, not against you. His desire is for you to prosper and be successful in everything you put your hands to.

God is greater than any problems you'll face today or against any situation you're dealing with. I've read the entire Bible through and through, and God has never lost a battle. He has a perfect record.

If you truly believed God is for you, how would that change how you live? Once you figure that out, then go do it.

151

THINK FOR A CHANGE

And now, dear brothers and sisters, one final thing. Fix your thoughts on what is true, and honorable, and right, and pure, and lovely, and admirable. Think about things that are excellent and worthy of praise.
Philippians 4:8

What you think about matters. Have you ever considered that not every thought that rolls through your brain originated with you? There's a war going on in your mind for your thought life. It's a battle between those of the Holy Spirit and those that are transplanted by the enemy. The problem is that the transplanted thoughts are lies, and they sound a lot like your thoughts, don't they? That's why it's important that we periodically think about what we think about.

Paul reminds us that we need to think about what is true and good. What do we know that is true and good? The answer is the Word of God. That's why it's important to know and meditate on the Word of God. As you begin to meditate on the Word of God, you'll start to think differently, and you'll have a renewed mind. It's your choice, so make it count.

152

WHEN JESUS IS SILENT

But Jesus gave her no reply, not even a word. Then his disciples urged him to send her away. "Tell her to go away," they said. "She is bothering us with all her begging."
Matthew 15:23

In this passage, a Gentile woman came to Jesus begging for help regarding her demon-possessed daughter. After her first request, she heard nothing from Jesus. At first glance, it looked like Jesus was being cruel, but a closer reading of the text reveals something different. The first time she came to Him, she was begging. The second time she came to Him, she was worshipping (Matt. 15:25). Jesus doesn't want you to beg; He wants you to worship.

Don't mistake Jesus' silence for a no. Some things just take worship.

153

SILENT SATURDAY

The women were terrified and bowed with their faces to the ground.
Then the men asked, "Why are you looking among the dead for
someone who is alive? He isn't here! He is risen from the dead!
Remember what he told you back in Galilee, that the Son of Man must
be betrayed into the hands of sinful men and be crucified, and that he
would rise again on the third day."
Luke 24:5-7

The day between Good Friday and Easter Sunday is known as Silent Saturday. Scripture records that Jesus was crucified on a Friday and raised to life again on the third day. There is no mention in the Gospels of God saying anything to His people in between the crucifixion and the resurrection. It was a day of silence.

There are moments in our lives where we might feel like heaven is silent, and we're not hearing anything. During these moments, we have to stand on God's promises and trust that God is still working amid our disappointments. Just because you're not seeing anything happen, doesn't mean God is not working. Regardless of how bad things look, He's still faithful to His Word.

154

DON'T BE AFRAID OF THE DARK

*Early on the first day of the week, while it was still dark, Mary
Magdalene went to the tomb and saw that the stone had been removed
from the entrance.*
John 20:1

Most children are afraid of the dark. The reason they are scared of the dark is that they cannot see clearly. When Mary Magdalene came to anoint the body of Jesus, she came while it was still dark. Truthfully, the past three days had been rough on her and the disciples. They were severely disappointed at the death of their beloved friend. Even though it was a dark situation, God's hands weren't tied. In fact, when the other disciples arrived at the tomb, they found the wrappings of Jesus' body lying there.

When things look dark in your life, it doesn't mean God's not working. Sometimes He does His best work in the dark!

SUIT UP FOR THE FIGHT

A final word: Be strong in the Lord and in his mighty power. Put on all of God's armor so that you will be able to stand firm against all strategies of the devil.
Ephesians 6:10-11

Paul instructs believers everywhere to put on all of God's armor so they can stand against the enemy. This verse isn't just a cute Sunday School lesson for children. It's a cry from the Apostle Paul to suit up for war. We face an unseen enemy whose sole purpose is to steal, kill, and destroy (John 10:10).

We must put on the armor of God every day, just as you would clean clothes. Don't leave your house inadequately clothed for the day. The armor of God will help you to stand firm against the enemy.

USE YOUR GIFT

God has given each of you a gift from his great variety of spiritual gifts. Use them well to serve one another.
1 Peter 4:10

Part of being a great leader is learning to encourage the people around you. If someone is breathing, they need encouragement! I'm not the greatest leader by any stretch of the imagination, but I've learned that encouraging others requires zero skills.

Who needs to be encouraged in your sphere of influence? Send them a text this morning, call them or handwrite them a note.

DON'T BE FOOLED!

Don't be fooled by those who say such things, for "bad company
corrupts good character."
1 Corinthians 15:33

Too many people approach relationships and friendships haphazardly. They'll allow anyone to influence and speak into their life. Life is too short to waste it hanging around the wrong people. There's nothing wrong with helping people, but when they start pulling you down, it's time to start cutting the fat.

Don't be fooled. Your relationships matter. Association brings assimilation. Who you follow will determine who you become.

158

AVOID SHORTCUTS

Then the devil took him up and revealed to him all the kingdoms of the world in a moment of time. "I will give you the glory of these kingdoms and authority over them," the devil said, "because they are mine to give to anyone I please. I will give it all to you if you will worship me."
Luke 4:5-7

In this passage, Satan offered Jesus a shortcut to avoid pain and suffering in His life. It was an old tactic for sure. The 'ole bait and switch deal! The devil offered Him the world in exchange for His worship.

Satan offers us the same deal today. He offers us the world in exchange for our worship. In essence, it's a shortcut for life. Jesus could have taken the deal, but it would have been a shortcut. He could have gained the authority of the world without going to the cross.

What's Christianity without the cross? It's no Christianity at all! Christianity without a cross is just another stale religion without a savior! Without the cross, there would be no resurrection. Without the resurrection, there is no hope or no promise of eternity with God. Yeah, it was a shortcut. Remember, not every shortcut is worth taking. Some are detours.

DON'T GIVE UP!

"But as for you, be strong and courageous, for your work will be rewarded."
2 Chronicles 15:7

In this passage, King Asa was in the midst of an organizational turn-around. Israel was in a mess spiritually, financially, numerically, and physically. It was a disaster for sure, but King Asa was determined to see Israel turn back to God.

During this time, King Asa had grown tired because of the enormous task of trying to turn Israel around. Still, a prophet came to him at just the right time and breathed new life into his mission.

Sometimes it's easy to get tired because of the work, but we must keep plodding along. The reward comes after the work. Be willing to stay at it as long as it takes. Some turnarounds just take time.

VISION LOSS

"All right," Nahash said, "but only on one condition. I will gouge out the right eye of every one of you as a disgrace to all Israel!"
1 Samuel 11:2

Compromise is a subtle enemy. It seduces you into letting your guard down and causes disgrace in your life. Compromising doesn't happen all at once. It happens slowly over time when we give in to the little things. We often rationalize the compromises because we fool ourselves into thinking that little sins aren't that big of a deal. One beer won't hurt you. One kiss won't kill you. One... (name your compromise).

Compromising with the enemy always results in the loss of vision. When you lose your vision, you'll also lose your way.

161

CONSECRATE YOURSELF

Then Joshua told the people, "Purify yourselves, for tomorrow the LORD
will do great wonders among you."
Joshua 3:5

Our job is to consecrate ourselves; the Lord's job is to do miracles. When we take the time to consecrate ourselves, we are devoting and committing ourselves to the Lord. As believers, it's easy to place pressure on ourselves to see miracles happen in our lives. A focus on personal consecration would bring better results. The best predictor of tomorrow's miracles is today's consecration.

PRACTICE MAKES CHAMPIONS

*When Abram heard that his nephew Lot had been captured, he
mobilized the 318 trained men who had been born into his household.
Then he pursued Kedorlaomer's army until he caught up with them
at Dan.*
Genesis 14:14

In this passage, Abram brought his 318 trained men and defeated four
kings. It was a miracle for sure, but don't neglect a small detail here.
Abram's men were not ordinary men; they were trained warriors. He
made them practice for war and combat when no one was looking. These
were some bad dudes. They made the Navy Seals look like Boy Scouts!

Champions prepare for success by training and practice. I prepare for
daily success by having a daily devotional habit. The night before, I make
sure my Bible, pen, and journal are laid out for my morning appoint-
ment. Preparing the night before has made it easier for me to develop this
habit in my life. I've never won a Super Bowl, but this daily exercise has
conditioned me to better run my race.

163

MAKE A GOOD DEPOSIT

A good person produces good things from the treasury of a good heart, and an
evil person produces evil things from the treasury of an evil heart. What you
say flows from what is in your heart.
Luke 6:45

Many people read this verse and only see the negative side, but there's a positive side as well. When you deposit good things into your heart, that's what will eventually come out. You can only make a withdrawal on that which you have deposited into your life. You can only withdraw good when you've taken the time to make good deposits. It might mean reading Scripture for a few minutes each day or listening to a podcast, or listening to some worship music. Either way, good can only produce good.

164

NO EXPIRATION DATE

Heaven and earth will disappear, but my words will never disappear.
Luke 21:33

There's nothing worse than drinking soured milk. If you drink it once, you'll never forget it. You've heard the old cliché, "Nothing last forever." This statement is almost true. This Scripture reminds us that one day God will make a new heaven and a new earth. He'll make a new heaven and earth because they'll eventually wear out like garments. However, God's Word never wears out! His Word never goes out of style.

The Word of God does not have an expiration date. It always stays fresh and alive. This is a good reminder that every time we speak out God's Word, it remains active into eternity and does not return to the Lord until it has achieved its set purpose (Isaiah 55:11). Keep speaking it!

WALK WITH THE WISE

Walk with the wise and become wise; associate with fools and get in trouble.
Proverbs 13:20

Show me your friends, and I will show you your future. You become who you associate with. You grow wise by learning from other leaders. Last year I read 36 books, and I'm reading more this year. I can't be around every great leader, but I can read their books. An excellent place to start with is the biographies of great leaders.

What books will you read this year? You'll only get what you plan for. I started keeping a reading list on my phone, and it has helped tremendously.

WALKING WITH GOD

Enoch lived 365 years, walking in close fellowship with God. Then one day he disappeared, because God took him.
Genesis 5:23-24

Enoch walked in close fellowship with God for 365 years before he was raptured. This is a good reminder that we need a daily encounter with God. One man's walk with God changed his family tree. I pray that my family will say that I walked with God as well.

NEW BATTLES REQUIRE NEW INSTRUCTIONS

But after a while the Philistines returned and again spread out across
the valley of Rephaim. And again David asked the LORD what to do.
"Do not attack them straight on," the LORD replied. "Instead, circle
around behind and attack them near the poplar trees."
2 Samuel 5:22-23

David never assumed the same thing would work twice. New battles require new instructions. Not long after David had been anointed as king of Israel, the Philistines attacked him. He swiftly defeated them and sent them home to lick their wounds and regroup, and then they attacked again.

They attacked David in the Valley of Rephaim (Giants). David had faced a giant many years ago as a young man, but these were new giants, and they would require new tactics. When facing new giants, you must take time to receive new marching orders from the Lord. David never assumed he knew what was best. When faced with this attack, the first thing he did was inquire of the Lord. Prayer was not his last resort; it was David's first response. Before all else fails, pray first!

THE ATTRACTION OF THE ANOINTING

When the Philistines heard that David had been anointed king of Israel, they mobilized all their forces to capture him. But David was told they were coming, so he went into the stronghold.

2 Samuel 5:17

After David had been anointed king over all of Israel, the enemy heard about it and came up in full force to attack him in the Valley of Rephaim (Valley of Giants). David went to the stronghold and sought the Lord. After hearing from the Lord, David defeated the enemy at Baal Perazim (God of Breakthrough). You might be in a valley of giants, but you serve a God of Breakthroughs! God will break out against your enemies today, and you'll walk in a breakthrough.

UNMET EXPECTATIONS

And while they were there, the time came for her baby to be born. She gave birth to her firstborn son. She wrapped him snugly in strips of cloth and laid him in a manger, because there was no lodging available for them.
Luke 2:6-7

The story of Jesus' birth was no Hallmark movie. He was birthed in a cave surrounded by animals where it smelled of animal dung and urine. A young mother would hardly dream of giving birth to her son in such a place! After giving birth to her son, she placed him in a manger, which is nothing more than a feeding trough. Mary saw a dirty feeding trough; God saw a bed fit for a King.

Sometimes when God doesn't meet our expectations, it just means He has something greater than we can understand or imagine. The key is to keep persevering. You can have hope this season in the midst of your pain because God is good and has great things in store for you.

170

DO WHAT IT SAYS

But don't just listen to God's word. You must do what it says. Otherwise, you are only fooling yourselves.
James 1:22

It's one thing to listen to the Word of God; it's quite another thing to do what it says. Most Christians do not need more knowledge; they need more obedience. If you're ever unsure of what to do, just do the next right thing. Believers often feel like they're not hearing from the Lord. It could be that they haven't done the last thing He instructed them to do. If you want more revelation from God, then you need to go back and do the last thing He told you to do. Obeyed revelation leads to more revelation.

THERE ARE NO DEAD ENDS

*Then the L*ORD *said to Moses, "Why are you crying out to me? Tell the people to get moving!"*
Exodus 14:15

This morning while walking, I saw a sign that read, "Dead End." Have you ever felt like you're at a dead-end? You are not the first person to feel that way, and you certainly won't be the last.

While fleeing from Egypt, the Israelites had this same feeling. After leaving Egypt, they faced Pharaoh's army on one side and the Red Sea on the other. During this moment, the Lord said to Moses, "Why are you crying out to me? Tell the Israelites to move on" (Exodus 14:15). They were paralyzed with fear because they could not see the possibilities in front of them. The Lord was about to part the sea for them to keep walking. As I saw the sign this morning, the Lord whispered, "It's only a dead end when you stop moving." A dead-end can be God's redirection if you will let it. If you're facing a dead end today, then find a way to keep moving. Ask God to let you see new possibilities.

SPEAK THE BLESSING

It was by faith that Isaac promised blessings for the future to his sons,
Jacob and Esau.
Hebrews 11:20

Jacob's sons were hardly the poster children of righteousness. Jacob was a deceiver, and Esau dishonored his parents by marrying the wrong woman. Despite this, they were still blessed by their father.

Isaac spoke a blessing over his sons not based on what he saw in the present but by what he wanted to see in their future. It takes faith to pray and speak over your children when you don't see what you want to see in their life. Sometimes children make bad decisions and do dumb things. Don't let their present situations dictate your faith in God and in what He can do in and through them.

The blessing came from the words he spoke over them. Our words matter! You have the power of life and death in your tongue. What do you speak over your children? Speak life, not death. If you need to, identify some scriptural promises to speak over your children.

DO THE WORK

Do you see any truly competent workers? They will serve kings rather than working for ordinary people.
Proverbs 22:29

The difference between doing what you want to do and what you need to do is discipline. Discipline is also the same character trait that will separate you from being average. It's easy to look at successful people in business, athletics, or their respective fields and think they got lucky. Most people aren't lucky; they're just more disciplined than you. Many people want to serve in high places, but if you're going to serve in a high place, you must develop your skills in a low place. When you treat low places like high places, the Lord can elevate you to high places.

174

BUILD YOUR HOME

A wise woman builds her home, but a foolish woman tears it down with
her own hands.
Proverbs 14:1

In this passage, the writer of Proverbs is comparing a wise woman to a foolish woman. A wise woman is smart enough to realize she can build up those in her house. She's learned that the best way to get the best out of her husband is by speaking life over him, rather than criticizing or dishonoring him. A foolish woman tears her household down when she belittles her husband or shames him in front of others.

Several years ago, I heard a profound statement by Pastor Jimmy Evans. He said, "Your marriage will never be better than your mouth." It's important to use your words to build up your house. Your family will be a reflection of your words. Build them up with your words; don't tear them down. If you haven't done a good job with them so far, then repent and start fresh today.

175

A DAILY DOSE OF ENCOURAGEMENT

You must warn each other every day, while it is still "today," so that none of you will be deceived by sin and hardened against God.
Hebrews 3:13

Encouragement is a lot like vitamins; they work best when they're taken daily. Ironically, the verse instructs us to encourage one another daily. Apparently, we leak because encouragement is something we constantly need. There are many ways to encourage someone, such as a text message, a written note, a pat on the back, a sincere compliment, or even a smile. Make a point of going out of your way to encourage someone today. Who will you encourage?

IT'S GOD'S BATTLE

*He said, "Listen, all you people of Judah and Jerusalem! Listen, King
Jehoshaphat! This is what the LORD says: Do not be afraid! Don't be
discouraged by this mighty army, for the battle is not yours, but God's."*
2 Chronicles 20:15

Judah was facing a vastly superior army. They were outnumbered and out
weaponed. It didn't look good for the home team, but God likes an
underdog story!

The only instructions the Lord gave Judah was to go out and face the
enemy. By the time Judah had marched out to the battlefield, the enemy
had already turned on each other and slaughtered one another. Judah
marched out for battle, but God had already handled the business by the
time they arrived. The only thing they had to do was pick up the plunder.
There was so much stuff that it took them three days to do it. That's not
bad for a day's work! Remember, when it's God's battle, the odds are in
your favor because He's undefeated.

THE DAY AND NIGHT BELONG TO GOD

Both day and night belong to you; you made the starlight and the sun.
You set the boundaries of the earth, and you made both summer and
winter.
Psalm 74:16-17

God made every season in which you find yourself. The night and the winter belong to Him as well. Nothing is going on in your life that God does not know about or has not passed through His divine filter. He's set boundaries on your life, and nothing gets past them without His divine approval. God is in control of your situation. It might be a dark night, but eventually, it will give way to the light of day. Every season is only temporary. Keep believing for God's best!

BE THANKFUL

Give thanks to the LORD, for he is good! His faithful love endures forever.
Psalm 107:1

Being thankful is an act of your will, not your emotions. The more you do it, the more you'll feel it. If you wait to be thankful when you feel it, there's a good chance it may never come.

One of the best ways to practice gratitude is by writing it down and keeping a journal. Several years ago, I kept a list in my journal entitled "My Blessings List." Whenever I felt like the Lord had blessed me with something or had done something in my life, I would record it in my journal. At times, I go back and read my list. This is so encouraging because I quickly realize that God had been really good to me.

Scientific studies have proven that people who regularly practice gratitude are healthier mentally and are more prone to happiness and joy in life. They've come to understand that gratitude is an act, not an emotion. You can develop gratitude in your life. The more you practice it, the easier it becomes for you.

FIGHT FOR YOUR FAMILY

The serpent was the shrewdest of all the wild animals the Lord God had made.
One day he asked the woman, "Did God really say you must not eat the fruit
from any of the trees in the garden?"
Genesis 3:1

The devil didn't show up in the Garden of Eden until there was a threat of multiplication. When Adam was by himself, he never had to deal with the devil. After Eve showed up and there was a threat of godly offspring, the devil sprang into action. He hates the family unit and the threat that unity with God means to him.

The devil spoke to Eve and tempted her with the fruit from the tree. Unfortunately, Adam was standing there and said nothing. Eve was deceived; Adam ate the fruit by choice. He should have laid hands on the snake and whipped him!

There will be times in your life when you're going to have to fight for your family. It might require you to speak up for them or to fight on your knees in prayer. Some things in your life are worth fighting for! Fight for your family.

180

YOU NEED GRACE AND TRUTH IN YOUR LIFE

For the law was given through Moses, but God's unfailing love and
faithfulness came through Jesus Christ.
John 1:17

The Law in the Old Testament was the truth, but it didn't allow much room for grace. In fact, the Law was so hard to follow that God required the priests to sacrifice a spotless lamb. The only way to deal with sins under the Law was to shed innocent blood.

In the New Testament, Jesus came as the spotless lamb, and He came with grace and truth. He always spoke the truth, but laced the truth with grace.

As believers, we need to speak the truth because it's the only way people will be set free, but we must do it with love. If you don't speak with love, no one wants to hear the truth. As Christians, we need to exemplify both truth and grace! They keep us balanced.

JUST SAY THE WORD!

I am not even worthy to come and meet you. Just say the word from
where you are, and my servant will be healed.
Luke 7:7

In this passage, a centurion had invited Jesus into his home to heal his servant. As Jesus approached his home, the centurion recognized his unworthiness to have a Jewish Rabbi come into the home of a Gentile. It would have been scandalous for Jesus to do so, resulting in Him being unclean afterward.

The centurion was faced with an impossibility, but he understood the power of the spoken word in a situation. When you personally know the Word, you can speak the Word. Your best response to your impossibility is to speak the Word over it. We have the promise of the Father that He's careful to watch over His Word and to perform it. When you don't know what to do, "Just say the Word!"

YOU'RE BEING TESTED

These are the nations that the LORD left in the land to test those Israelites who had not experienced the wars of Canaan. He did this to teach warfare to generations of Israelites who had no experience in battle. These are the nations: the Philistines (those living under the five Philistine rulers), all the Canaanites, the Sidonians, and the Hivites living in the mountains of Lebanon from Mount Baal-hermon to Lebo-hamath.

Judges 3:1-3

The Lord intentionally left some enemy nations in Israel so that the newer generation would know how to handle war and adversity. People rarely grow through comfort. Pain and experience are still the best teachers.

Maybe the enemies you're facing today were left there by God to prepare you for your next season. Today's problems become tomorrow's platforms!

183

REHEARSALS ARE IMPORTANT

I have done this to both lions and bears, and I'll do it to this pagan Philistine, too, for he has defied the armies of the living God!
1 Samuel 17:36

Weddings have rehearsals. Plays and productions have rehearsals. Rehearsals are essential because they prepare you for the big day. They serve as times of preparation so when you're in a position where you have to perform publicly, you know how to act.

When David was faced with a giant, he encouraged himself by thinking back to past battles. He had fought a lion and bear and had survived. Sure, it was scary and dangerous, but he chose to focus on his victories, not his hurts. Faith chooses to rehearse your victories, not your hurts.

IF YOU CAN BELIEVE

"What do you mean, 'If I can'?" Jesus asked. "Anything is possible if a person believes." The father instantly cried out, "I do believe, but help me overcome my unbelief!"
Mark 9:23-24

For years, my prayers were small because they reflected the narrative I believed about God. I was afraid to ask for anything big because I had limiting beliefs. At times, I felt like I was bothering Him, or that He wouldn't do it for me. Unconsciously, I had an orphan mentality regarding how I came to my Heavenly Father.

However, I've come to the realization that I've been adopted as one of His sons, and that makes me an heir along with Jesus. I've been grafted into God's family with all the rights and privileges as those of Jesus. Also, I now realize that it doesn't take any more energy to think big than it does to think small. You might as well think big. In this passage, the father was honest with Jesus and asked for help with his unbelief. There are times when we need to say, "Lord, enlarge my vision!" If your vision for your life doesn't scare you, it's probably not big enough!

185

GOD LOVES YOU

And a voice from heaven said, "This is my dearly loved Son, who brings
me great joy."
Matthew 3:17

It's easy to fall into the trap of thinking we can earn God's love or do something to deserve it. Frankly, there's nothing we could ever do to earn God's love or to make Him love us more than He already does. God's affirmation of Jesus came before the cross, not after it. God loved and affirmed Jesus even before He did His first miracle. God feels the same about you. You can never do anything to make Him love you more than He does right now.

186

PRAYING THE SCRIPTURES

Study this Book of Instruction continually. Meditate on it day and night so you will be sure to obey everything written in it. Only then will you prosper and succeed in all you do.
Joshua 1:8

The only way to keep the Bible on your lips is to speak it and pray it. Praying the Scriptures will change your prayer life. There are times in your life when you don't know what to pray. When this happens, you have two options. First, if you're baptized in the Holy Spirit, you can pray in the Spirit (Romans 8:26-27). Second, you can pray the Scriptures. When you pray the Scriptures, you know you're praying God's will. When what He wants becomes what you want, you will always get what you want.

187

EVEN MORE FRUITFUL

"I am the true grapevine, and my Father is the gardener. He cuts off every branch of mine that doesn't produce fruit, and he prunes the branches that do bear fruit so they will produce even more."
John 15:1-2

If you've ever tried to grow shrubs or fruit trees, then you understand the necessity of trimming back the old, dead branches. Often, the branches become so heavy with dead fruit that they must be trimmed. The trimming is necessary for new growth. Likewise, God sometimes cuts off the dead places in our lives. The pruning process can be painful but it is necessary for our growth. If He's pruning you, it's because He's got more fruit for you.

188

DON'T BUY THE LIE!

I prayed to the Lord, and he answered me. He freed me from all my fears.
Psalm 34:4

The biggest lie of the enemy is that God doesn't care. The second biggest lie is that God doesn't listen. The devil sits on a throne of lies! (I borrowed that quote from a particular Christmas movie!) The devil is also the father of lies (John 8:44) and lying in his native tongue.

You have to believe that God cares, God listens, and God responds. The key is seeking the Lord. When you turn toward Him, He turns towards you. "Come close to God, and God will come close to you" (James 4:8).

189

DON'T LET ANGER STEW

And "don't sin by letting anger control you." Don't let the sun go down while
you are still angry, for anger gives a foothold to the devil.
Ephesians 4:26-27

Being angry is not a sin. The key is not sinning with your anger. There are times when we need to display righteous anger, especially when we see injustice around us. When Jesus walked into the temple and saw the money changers, He drove them out with a whip and flipped tables.

There are also times when we must be careful and not let anger ruin a relationship. Anger is like soup, it is served best when it has had time to stew. Don't let it stew in your relationships. When you let anger stew too long, you can unknowingly give the devil a foothold in your life. Anger left unchecked grows to bitterness. Bitterness starts as a small root, but it grows into an unyielding vine that defiles many. The best time to deal with anger is yesterday. The second best time is now.

190

USE YOUR SWORD

As a result, Joshua overwhelmed the army of Amalek in battle.
Exodus 17:13

Joshua overcame a superior army in an unconventional way. While he was in the valley fighting, Moses was on the hill praying. Even though Moses was praying and interceding on Joshua's behalf, it still required Joshua to use his sword.

Times have changed over the years, and very few armies go out to battle with swords anymore. Even though times have changed, one thing that has not changed is the Word of God. It's still as powerful today as it was in Joshua's day.

If you're fighting a battle today, don't neglect your sword. Your sword is the Word of God (Ephesians 6:17). Every time you speak it and pray it, you're swinging your sword against a hidden enemy. It takes a supernatural weapon to defeat a supernatural enemy. Don't neglect your sword!

191

THANKSGIVING IS THE WAY

Enter his gates with thanksgiving; go into his courts with praise. Give thanks to him and praise his name.

Psalm 100:4

There's a progressive path into the presence of the Lord. According to this verse, we go through His gates with thanksgiving. Your thanksgiving will give way to praise, and it's your praise that will get you into His throne room. Do you see a progression here? It's not a formula per se, but it's a good reminder that we shouldn't just rush into His presence, demanding our way. That would be rude.

When you don't know what to say to the Lord, you can always start with, "Thank you." It's always a good place to start.

DON'T BE AFRAID TO START SMALL

*Do not despise these small beginnings, for the L*ORD *rejoices to see the work begin, to see the plumb line in Zerubbabel's hand.*
Zechariah 4:10

God is not afraid of our small beginnings. He seems to enjoy it more than we do. Maybe it's because it requires a level of intimacy and trust in Him that we normally don't display.

A lot of people are afraid to start something new because it requires a risk. Starting something new also assumes there is the potential for failure. Years ago, I was afraid to write. I was afraid to give myself permission to be a beginner. As silly as it sounds, it's easy to look at the success of others and compare yourself to them. At times, I have been tempted to compare myself to Max Lucado or Mark Batterson. It would be tempting to say, "I could never write like them!" In reality, they started just like I did —with one word on a page. Never compare your beginning to someone else's middle, and never let the size of your start determine the size of your vision.

193

GOD OWNS IT ALL

But I do not need the bulls from your barns or the goats from your pens.
For all the animals of the forest are mine, and I own the cattle on a
thousand hills.
Psalm 50:9-10

God doesn't need anything from us. He's without need and without want. In fact, He owns the cattle on a thousand hills. That's a lot of cattle. For that matter, He owns the hills and the dirt, too! If you have a need, tell God about it. If He has to, He could sell a few cattle to meet your need. So, there you have it. Good reminder for today!

YOU BE YOU!

Then Saul gave David his own armor—a bronze helmet and a coat of mail. David put it on, strapped the sword over it, and took a step or two to see what it was like, for he had never worn such things before. "I can't go in these," he protested to Saul. "I'm not used to them." So David took them off again.
1 Samuel 17:38-39

When David was about to go out and face the giant, King Saul encouraged him to put on his personal armor. It could have been because David was about to fight a giant without armor. It also could have been because Saul was hoping that if David killed the giant while wearing his armor that Saul would somehow get the credit for it. Either way, Saul's armor didn't fit David.

Likewise, every time we try to be someone we are not, we do the same thing as David did. We need to learn to be satisfied with our own gifts, our own callings, our own personalities, and our own weapons. I suspect David would have looked ridiculous walking around in Saul's armor because it would have been too big for him. Saul was one of the tallest men in Israel, and David, a teenage boy at the time. Don't wear Saul's armor when God has called you to be a David.

FIND STRENGTH IN THE LORD

When David and his men saw the ruins and realized what had happened to their families, they wept until they could weep no more. David's two wives, Ahinoam from Jezreel and Abigail, the widow of Nabal from Carmel, were among those captured. David was now in great danger because all his men were very bitter about losing their sons and daughters, and they began to talk of stoning him. But David found strength in the LORD his God.
1 Samuel 30:3-6

While David and his men were off serving the Lord, the enemy came in and ambushed his camp. The Amalekites came in and took everything. They took their stuff, their wives, and their children. To make matters worse, David's men were so discouraged they were ready to take out their frustrations on David by stoning him to death. Talk about a bad day!

Have you ever found yourself having that kind of day? I suspect you have. David's response to his crisis was surprising. You'll notice he was honest with his emotions and his feelings of loss. He wept until he couldn't weep anymore. After his cryfest, he wouldn't let himself continue to wallow in self-pity. He finally had to take a moment and encourage himself in the Lord. How did David encourage himself in the Lord?

I believe it was by doing two things. First, I think David worshipped the Lord. When he worshipped the Lord, he got his eyes off his circumstances and on to God's glory. Second, he remembered all the times God had helped him in the past. David's past victories gave him courage for today's struggles. After David encouraged himself in the Lord, he turned around and cast the same vision to his men. They would eventually go after the enemy and get all their stuff back with interest. The devil can steal your stuff, but he can't steal your praise. Eventually, you'll get your stuff back with interest.

STORE YOUR TREASURES IN HEAVEN

Store your treasures in heaven, where moths and rust cannot destroy,
and thieves do not break in and steal.
Matthew 6:20

I have some bad news for you. You're not getting out of this world alive. Unless we're raptured, we are all going to die. There's more to life than this life.

We spend an excessive amount of time trying to hold on to things. It's incredible how many storage rental facilities we have in our area. Recently I was driving to a nearby city and was shocked to see the large number of storage facilities in the area. Most of those units are full of stuff that is just sitting there—not being used and just rotting away. Unfortunately, we've bought into the idea that things will make us happy.

On the other hand, the Bible teaches us that we need to store up treasures in heaven. Every time we give to a missionary, an orphan, or a homeless person, we are storing up our treasure in heaven. The Bible teaches us that God keeps good records. He will pay us back for the good we do. What are you storing up for yourself in heaven?

GOD LOVES YOU

But God showed his great love for us by sending Christ to die for us while we were still sinners.
Romans 5:8

I have come to the simple truth that God's love is greater than my sin. God loved you while you were still a mess. It's easy to love people who love us and who have it all together. On the other hand, it's hard to love people who are "Extra Grace Required" (EGR) kind of people. We've all met people who we would describe as "EGR" kind of people. Before God transformed your life, you were an "EGR" person. You're probably still a mess, but God still loves your mess!

198

KEEP STANDING!

Therefore, put on every piece of God's armor so you will be able to resist the enemy in the time of evil. Then after the battle you will still be standing firm.
Ephesians 6:13

There are times in life when you must stand your ground. It might mean standing for truth or standing up against injustice. It might mean doing the right thing even when it hurts or when no one else will. Doing the right thing is rarely easy, and you're usually in the minority when you do it. There are also times in your life when all you can do is all you can do. When this happens, drive a stake in the ground and take a stand. After you take your stand, trust God for the rest.

199

THE ODDS ARE IN YOUR FAVOR!

What shall we say about such wonderful things as these? If God is for
us, who can ever be against us?
Romans 8:31

There are moments in life when we are going to feel outnumbered and overwhelmed. Truthfully, there are times that suffering comes our way, and we cannot escape it. Despite all of this, we can remember the words of Paul when he reminds us that God is for us. Think about that! God is for you, not against you! Don't buy the lie that the enemy is selling. God is not mad at you, and you're not being punished for your sin. If you're born again, the price for your sin has already been paid. Remember, God is on your side, and His team is stacked!

200

PUT ON THE TOWEL

Jesus knew that the Father had given him authority over everything and that he had come from God and would return to God.
John 13:3

In first-century Israel, households commonly had servants. The servant would prepare the meal as well as wash the feet of guests as they entered the home. People walked most places, and their feet often got dirty, especially as they walked along the same roads the animals walked on. You can surmise the types of droppings that people would walk on along the road. Washing the feet of guests was a dirty job.

The host expressed honor and respect for his guests by making sure someone washed their feet. A person of high stature or a Rabbi would not wash peoples' feet. Frankly, they considered this role as beneath them. However, Jesus could serve in the role of a servant because He understood whose He was, and He understood His purpose. Nothing is beneath you when you know who is above you. How can you serve someone today?

201

STAY FOCUSED!

"Yes, come," Jesus said. So Peter went over the side of the boat and walked on the water toward Jesus. But when he saw the strong wind and the waves, he was terrified and began to sink. "Save me, Lord!" he shouted. Jesus immediately reached out and grabbed him. "You have so little faith," Jesus said. "Why did you doubt me?"
Matthew 14:29-31

As many faults as Peter had, he was still the only disciple to walk on water. I suspect that many years later, Peter would sit around reminiscing with the other disciples about how he was the only one to walk on water. I suspect John also reminded him that he was also the only one to sink!

Peter did walk on water, and it was because he focused his attention on the Water Walker rather than on the storm. The moment he began to focus his attention on the wind was the moment he began to sink.

When storms come our way, it's easy to focus on the calamity around us rather than on the Prince of Peace. If you're facing a storm today, I would encourage you to take the time to focus on Jesus and look for His hand. He's in your storm, and He's reaching out to catch you. Sometimes Jesus calms your storms; other times, He gives you the ability to walk over them.

DON'T DO IT!

Hot-tempered people must pay the penalty. If you rescue them once, you will have to do it again.
Proverbs 19:19

Some lessons can only be learned the hard way. The famous theologian, John Wayne, once said, "If you're going to be dumb, you better be tough!"

As a parent, I often find myself wanting to fix things for my children. Truthfully, it pains me to see them struggle, but deep down, I know the struggle is good for them. The struggle will help them develop their perseverance and faith muscles. Likewise, when they get into trouble, we need to let them deal with the consequences and feel the pain of it. If we do it for them, we doom them to repeating the same mistake twice. Pain has a long memory. It keeps us from making the same mistake twice.

SURVIVING THE WILDERNESS

Then Jesus was led by the Spirit into the wilderness to be tempted there by the devil. For forty days and forty nights he fasted and became very hungry.
Matthew 4:1-2

The Israelites spent 40 years in the wilderness (Joshua 5:6). What should have been an 11-day journey turned into a 40-year delay. Their wilderness was never meant to be a destination; it was only supposed to be a layover on their way to the Promised Land.

Years later, Jesus would find himself in the wilderness as well. His experience only lasted 40 days, and He fasted during this time.

The wilderness often signifies the place between the old and the new things God is doing in your life. The wilderness is only meant to be a pathway of transition, not a destination. If you're in a desert right now, it just means you're headed to something new. The important thing is to continue to be led by the Holy Spirit and don't do anything that will disqualify you for your next season. That happened to Israel, but thankfully, it didn't happen to Jesus. He didn't allow the temptations of the moment to derail what God wanted to do in His future.

TRUST THE PROMISER

Two of the men who had explored the land, Joshua son of Nun and Caleb son of Jephunneh, tore their clothing. They said to all the people of Israel, "The land we traveled through and explored is a wonderful land! And if the LORD is pleased with us, he will bring us safely into that land and give it to us. It is a rich land flowing with milk and honey. Do not rebel against the LORD, and don't be afraid of the people of the land. They are only helpless prey to us! They have no protection, but the LORD is with us! Don't be afraid of them!"
Numbers 14:6-9

Before entering the Promised Land, Moses sent out a reconnaissance team of twelve spies. They were supposed to be the best of the best. They went and explored the land for forty days and returned with their report. Unfortunately, ten of the twelve spies gave a negative report. They focused on the size of their giants rather than on the size of their God.

If God could deliver them from Egypt, then surely, He could deliver them from these giants. The only problem was that the Israelites had forgotten about what God did to deliver them from Egypt. If you're going to possess your Promised Land, you must have greater faith in your Promiser than in your giants.

KEEP GETTING UP!

The godly may trip seven times, but they will get up again. But one disaster is enough to overthrow the wicked.
Proverbs 24:16

Babe Ruth is arguably one of the greatest baseball players in history. At one point, he held the record of 714 home runs. Few people also realize he struck out 1,330 times. He struck out almost twice as much as he hit home runs. You could see him as a failure, but he understood he had to be willing to strike out more to achieve that many home runs.

At some point in your life, you're going to strike out. If you're not failing, you're not trying. Failing is progress, if you fail forward. You're not a failure, if you learned from it. You're a learner, not a failure. You're not defeated until you quit. Get back up and keep swinging for the fence!

GOD'S PURPOSE IS GREATER THAN YOUR PAIN

The Lord will work out his plans for my life—for your faithful love, O Lord, endures forever. Don't abandon me, for you made me.
Psalm 138:8

It's too easy to look on Facebook or Instagram and see the pictures of all your friends and co-workers who seem like they're having their best life now. In reality, social media is a façade. We don't see people's struggles. We only see their highlight reels. Highlight reels are fun to watch, but they're only a snapshot of someone's life.

God's purpose for your life is greater than your pain. He will not abandon you or forsake you. He will never give up on you. If you're struggling today, it's just evidence of God working in your life.

If you're struggling today, you need to press pause and read this verse again and make it your daily declaration. God will fulfill His purpose for your life, and it's not predicated on your circumstances.

DON'T TAKE THE BAIT!

Don't answer the foolish arguments of fools, or you will become as foolish as they are. Be sure to answer the foolish arguments of fools, or they will become wise in their own estimation.
Proverbs 26:4-5

The famous humorist George Bernard Shaw once said, "I learned long ago, never to wrestle with a pig. You get dirty, and besides, the pig likes it." Wrestling with a pig is the same as answering a fool.

When dealing with a fool, it's best to show restraint and say nothing rather than try to defend yourself. Sometimes the best response is no response. Some people are just looking for an argument. Just because you're invited to an argument, doesn't mean you should attend. It's not worth responding to everyone! When you argue with a fool, you sink to their level. Don't take the bait!

208

REPAIR THE ALTAR

Then Elijah called to the people, "Come over here!" They all crowded around him as he repaired the altar of the LORD that had been torn down.
1 Kings 18:30

As I read about Elijah this morning, this verse caught my attention. The prophet Elijah called the people of Israel to himself. In their presence, He repaired the broken and unused altar.

A few verses later, the fire of God fell and consumed everything. I can't help but think maybe the Lord is waiting on His people to repair the broken altars and places in their lives before they can see true revival in their churches. True repentance precedes the miraculous.

What do you need to repent of this morning? What altar needs repairing in your life?

YOU HAVE TO PROVE YOURSELF

"Again, the Kingdom of Heaven can be illustrated by the story of a man going on a long trip. He called together his servants and entrusted his money to them while he was gone. He gave five bags of silver to one, two bags of silver to another, and one bag of silver to the last—dividing it in proportion to their abilities. He then left on his trip."
Matthew 25:14-15

Many people read this parable and think the master was being unfair when he gave each servant a different amount of gold to manage. He gave one servant five bags of gold. He gave another two bags, and the last servant received one bag. It would be easy to feel sorry for the last servant because he didn't get as much as the other servants.

When you look at this parable through the eyes of the master, you see things differently. The master didn't give the servants what they wanted but rather what they could manage. He gave to them based on their proven ability. What's unfair is to give someone more than he or she can effectively manage. What was meant to be a blessing for someone could destroy them. You've heard countless stories of children who received too much too soon, and it ends up destroying their life.

While we're talking about giving and managing finances, let me throw this out there as well. If you won't tithe on what you have, you won't tithe on what you want. You have to prove yourself with your current responsibilities before you're given more responsibilities.

WHEN YOU'RE NOT THE FIRST PICK

But the Lord *said to Samuel, "Don't judge by his appearance or height, for I have rejected him. The* Lord *doesn't see things the way you see them. People judge by outward appearance, but the* Lord *looks at the heart."*
1 Samuel 16:7

As a football fan, most people would agree that Tom Brady is arguably one of the greatest quarterbacks to play the game. Like him or not, he still has 7 Super Bowl rings, which is more than any other quarterback. The most interesting part of his story is that he was not a first-round draft pick. In fact, he was picked in the sixth round and drafted 199th overall. At the time, he was a no-name quarterback from the University of Michigan. There were six other quarterbacks picked ahead of him. Apparently, the professional scouts didn't see his potential.

King David wasn't the first pick either. He was an eighth-round draft pick. As the youngest son, he was the last pick. The good news is that while man looks at the outside, God always starts with what's on the inside. Don't worry about being everyone's first pick. If you feel over-looked, you're in good company. Wait for your turn!

211

GOD HAS MORE STORED UP FOR YOU

How great is the goodness you have stored up for those who fear you. You lavish it on those who come to you for protection, blessing them before the watching world.
Psalm 31:19

I love this verse because it reminds us of the generosity and goodness of God. God doesn't keep things from us; He keeps things for us. He stores up good things for us. He has things stored up just for you, and He blesses you right in front of others. Your only job is to obey and fear the Lord. Your job is obedience; then leave the results up to Him.

212

GOD ALLOWS DO-OVERS!

The faithful love of the LORD never ends! His mercies never cease. Great is his faithfulness; his mercies begin afresh each morning.
Lamentations 3:22-23

One of the best comedic movies of the early '90s was Groundhog Day. In the movie, actor Bill Murray portrays Phil Connors, a cynical television show weatherman covering the annual Groundhog Day event in Punxsutawney, Pennsylvania, who became trapped in a time loop, forcing him to relive February 2 repeatedly. After many bad days of repeating the same mistakes, Phil finally decides to use his knowledge of the loop to change himself and others: he saves people from deadly accidents and misfortunes. He also learns to play the piano, sculpt ice, and speak French.

Likewise, God's faithfulness in your life has no end. His faithfulness is ongoing, and His mercy never stops. I'm thankful God allows do-overs. Some days we need one. Every morning that you get up is a gift from God to try again.

213

PARTIAL OBEDIENCE IS DISOBEDIENCE

"But I did obey the Lord*," Saul insisted. "I carried out the mission he gave me. I brought back King Agag, but I destroyed everyone else. Then my troops brought in the best of the sheep, goats, cattle, and plunder to sacrifice to the* Lord *your God in Gilgal."*
1 Samuel 15:20-21

Earlier in this passage, the Lord instructed Saul to go and destroy all of the Amalekites and not spare anything that belonged to them. Before you think God was too harsh, you need to double back and read the entire chapter. The Amalekites were the vilest, cutthroat tribe in the Old Testament. While Israel was limping out of Egypt, the Amalekites swooped in and attacked them in their vulnerability. The Lord didn't punish the Amalekites for it then, but He vowed to punish them later when the time was right.

All Saul had to do was destroy everything, but instead, he caved to the peer pressure of his men and spared the best cattle and sheep so they could make a sacrifice to God. They also spared King Agag. (That was a mistake because Haman, from the book of Esther, was his descendant). By most standards, we would say Saul was obedient, except for these two things. Surely God wouldn't be angry at Saul for wanting to make a sacrifice? Actually, yes! Yes, He would.

Why? God understands that partial obedience is still disobedience. We cannot choose which of God's commandments and laws we want to obey. It's all or nothing in the Kingdom of God. In the end, Saul's partial obedience cost him his kingdom. If you're being partially obedient in an area of your life, it's time you go all in.

STANDING FIRM THROUGH THE STORM

When the storms of life come, the wicked are whirled away, but the godly have
a lasting foundation.
Proverbs 10:25

It rains on the just and the unjust (Matthew 5:45). At one point, everyone is going to face a storm in life. The difference between the righteous and the unrighteous is who will be standing when the storm has passed by. Storms are only temporary in your life, but righteous people are immovable. You can stand firm because the Lord is with you, and He's never forgotten or forsaken you. He's the original Rock and the chief cornerstone. He's unmovable!

GOD IS IN CONTROL

God says, "At the time I have planned, I will bring justice against the wicked. When the earth quakes and its people live in turmoil, I am the one who keeps its foundations firm. Interlude "I warned the proud, 'Stop your boasting!' I told the wicked, 'Don't raise your fists! Don't raise your fists in defiance at the heavens or speak with such arrogance.'" For no one on earth—from east or west, or even from the wilderness—should raise a defiant fist. It is God alone who judges; he decides who will rise and who will fall.
Psalm 75:2-7

This is such an encouraging Psalm! The writer reminds us that God is the one who chooses the appointed time for everything. He's not caught off guard or surprised by situations that surprise us. He's not up pacing the hallways in heaven. He's not losing sleep at night or worried about what to do next. He's the one that holds the pillars of the earth together.

Even when things feel out of control, we can rest assured knowing God controls every situation. No matter what happens, God is in control.

216

THE POWER OF LIFE AND DEATH ARE IN THE TONGUE

The tongue can bring death or life; those who love to talk will reap the
consequences.
Proverbs 18:21

While at lunch, I recently overheard a lady talking to another lady about a child she knew. She said, "He's the stupidest kid I've ever met!" They both got a good laugh about it. I don't know who the child was, but my heart broke for him. I could only imagine what this child has heard from people like this.

The Bible reminds us that we can use our words to bring life or death to other people. Today, let's choose life with our words.

GOD KNOWS YOUR NAME!

He counts the stars and calls them all by name.
Psalm 147:4

It's hard to imagine, but God knows how many stars there are, and He knows each of them by name! According to some scientists, the number of stars in a galaxy varies, but assuming an average of 100 billion stars per galaxy means there are about 1,000,000,000,000,000,000,000 (that's 1 billion trillion) stars in the observable universe! That's only the stars we can observe with our eyes.

If God has the stars numbered and named, then He knows YOU and your needs. He has you today! Be blessed!

GOD WILL FULFILL HIS PURPOSE FOR YOU

I cry out to God Most High, to God who will fulfill his purpose for me.
Psalm 57:2

It's reassuring to know that the only person who can thwart the purposes of God for your life is you. You can thwart His purpose by your disobedience, but as long as you try to serve God and do the right thing, you can trust that He knows what He's doing. There's nothing the enemy or any person can do to thwart the purposes of God for your life. If you're submitted to Him, God will help you to fulfill your life purpose. You don't have to worry; you won't leave this rock one day sooner until He is ready for you to!

219

FORGIVENESS IS EASIER THAN MATH!

Then Peter came to him and asked, "Lord, how often should I forgive someone who sins against me? Seven times?" "No, not seven times," Jesus replied, "but seventy times seven!"
Matthew 18:21-22

Forgiveness is easy until you have to do it. Forgiving is also easier than keeping score. Truthfully, forgiving someone is hard, especially when you did nothing to deserve it, such as when a spouse walks out on you or when someone betrays you. It could be when someone harmed you in some way.

Forgiveness is a choice you make and not something you feel like doing. When you willingly forgive others, it sets you free—not the person who hurt you. You forgive for your own sake, not for the sake of others. When you forgive others, then God will forgive you.

220

PRAY FIRST!

Seek the Kingdom of God above all else, and live righteously, and he will give you everything you need.
Matthew 6:33

Too often, seeking God in prayer is an afterthought rather than our first thought. Over the years, I've heard people say, "When all else fails, pray." What if we flipped the script and started saying, "Before anything else, pray first"?

Several years ago, I found myself dealing with a challenging situation that went on for a few weeks. In a moment of desperation, I cried out to the Lord and said, "Would you do something?" After I muttered those words, I heard the still small voice of the Holy Spirit saying, "You never asked before today." For a moment, I sat there in shock because I realized I had never prayed about this particular situation. For two weeks straight, all I did was complain about it and attempt to handle it myself. That very day, the problem was resolved. God won't answer prayers you don't pray.

GOD IN THE FLESH

he humbled himself in obedience to God and died a criminal's death on a cross.
Philippians 2:8

Jesus humbled himself when He left heaven to come to earth. Talk about downsizing! That was quite the move. In theological circles, this is known as the incarnation.

The incarnation of Christ is one of the greatest expressions of God's love for us in that we couldn't come to Him, so He came to us. He crossed Heaven and Earth to be with us. Know that you are loved today, because Jesus was dying to meet you!

222

DON'T BE SURPRISED

"I have told you all this so that you may have peace in me. Here on earth you will have many trials and sorrows. But take heart, because I have overcome the world."
John 16:33

Jesus wasn't trying to be negative; He was just being honest. As followers of Jesus, we are going to have trouble. It should come as no surprise to us.

I'm not sure why any of us are surprised by the moral depravity of this world. People do what comes naturally to them until Jesus saves them. The Good News is that He has overcome the world, and greater is He that is in us than he that is in the world. Go live it today, because we are not a people without hope. Our hope is in Jesus, not a politician, a position, or any other person!

223

SPIRITUAL DEHYDRATION

The instructions of the LORD are perfect, reviving the soul. The decrees of the LORD are trustworthy, making wise the simple.
Psalm 19:7

Dehydration can be deadly. The lack of water in our bodies can cause severe damage. Dehydration is subtle. Many people walk around every day dehydrated. It causes us to feel sluggish, lack energy, and be in a brain fog. Likewise, it's also a subtle thing to walk around spiritually dehydrated. The Word of God is not meant to drain you of life; it's meant to bring you life. If you need refreshing in your soul, you can get it from reading the Word of God. It's the Powerade for your spirit. If you're tired and sluggish today, an excellent place to start is with the water of life, and His name is Jesus!

THE FOOTSTOOL OF GOD

This is what the Lord says: "Heaven is my throne, and the earth is my footstool..."
Isaiah 66:1

God is bigger than we can imagine. Heaven and earth cannot contain Him. This Scripture reminds us that heaven is His throne, and the earth is His footstool. It's a good depiction of the power and glory of God. God is not worried or fretting regarding what is going on today. He's seated and in control today, and He's comfortable with the way things are headed. He's so pleased that His feet are propped up with the earth.

God is over what keeps you under! No problem or difficulty is too big for Him. Keep believing and praying for your miracle, for there is nothing He cannot do. God cannot and will not be stopped.

225

YOUR PRAYER HAS BEEN HEARD

But the angel said, "Don't be afraid, Zechariah! God has heard your prayer. Your wife, Elizabeth, will give you a son, and you are to name him John."
Luke 1:13

Zechariah and Elizabeth were childless and had prayed for years for a son. Most people would have given up on their miracle, but not Zechariah. By the time the angel visited him, "They had no children because Elizabeth was unable to conceive, and they were both very old." (Luke 1:7). To put it plainly, they were both past their childbearing years.

This hopeless situation was a perfect opportunity for a miracle. If you're in a desperate situation, then you're a prime candidate for a miracle. As long as you have a prayer, you have a chance! Your prayers do not have expiration dates. Keep praying until you see the answer.

226

GOD LIKES LEFTOVERS

They all ate as much as they wanted, and afterward, the disciples picked up twelve baskets of leftovers. About 5,000 men were fed that day, in addition to all the women and children!

Matthew 14:20-21

Jesus fed 5,000 men, plus their families (about 20,000 people), with five loaves and two fish. By the time it was all said and done, everyone had eaten until they were full, and they ended with more than what they started with. They started with five loaves and two fish, and they ended with twelve basketfuls of leftovers.

Before Jesus could bless and multiple it, the bread and fish had to be placed in His hands. So often, we want to see Jesus bless and multiply the things in our hands while we are still holding on to them. This is not the way it works in the Kingdom. In the Kingdom of God, it's faith that pleases God (Hebrews 11:6). God can't bless what you're not giving. It's only after the seed is sown that it can multiple. There's enough of God's provision and goodness to go around. There are no shortages in the Kingdom. In fact, He likes leftovers!

YOU NEED TO HAVE A BREAK-UP

Then he said to the crowd, "If any of you wants to be my follower, you must give up your own way, take up your cross daily, and follow me. If you try to hang on to your life, you will lose it. But if you give up your life for my sake, you will save it. And what do you benefit if you gain the whole world but are yourself lost or destroyed?"
Luke 9:23-25

If you're going to go all-in with Jesus, it's not going to be easy. It involves taking up your cross, which is intended to put to death the flesh. God's goal is to bring us new life, but we have to die to our flesh for that to happen. We have to die to our flesh because it is at war with what our spirit wants. Paul described the struggle this way, "I don't really understand myself, for I want to do what is right, but I don't do it. Instead, I do what I hate" (Romans 7:15). The greatest apostle in the New Testament is saying this! If he struggled with his flesh, I suspect most people do, too.

Taking up your cross is a daily exercise, not a one-time event. It involves the daily decision to submit to His will and His Kingdom. It means praying the prayer of, "Yet I want your will to be done, not mine." (Luke 22:42). If you want to be all in with Jesus, you have to have a breakup. You have to break up with the world.

228

DON'T LOSE HEART

And have you forgotten the encouraging words God spoke to you as his
children? He said, "My child, don't make light of the Lord's discipline, and don't
give up when he corrects you. For the Lord disciplines those he loves, and he
punishes each one he accepts as his child."
Hebrews 12:5-6

Parents discipline children for their good. Discipline refines character, and if done correctly, it keeps them on the right path of life. Typically, parents only discipline their own children. They don't discipline other people's children because they don't have the same relationship with them. Likewise, the Lord corrects us as His children because He loves us and has a relationship with us. If we aren't careful, we can misinterpret correction and buy into the lie that correction is God's rejection. Correction is not rejection; it's for your protection. If God is correcting you, it's because He loves you and believes in your potential.

STOP COMPLAINING!

Do everything without complaining and arguing, so that no one can criticize you. Live clean, innocent lives as children of God, shining like bright lights in a world full of crooked and perverse people.
Philippians 2:14-15

Complaining rarely changes anything. In most cases, complaining is a reflection of an ungrateful heart.

If you have time to complain about it, you have time to pray about it. One choice can lead to change; the other can't. I'll let you decide the better choice.

THIRD DAY MIRACLES

The next day there was a wedding celebration in the village of Cana in Galilee. Jesus' mother was there, and Jesus and his disciples were also invited to the celebration.

John 2:1-2

In the Bible, some miracles happened on the third day. Turning the water into wine was the first miracle Jesus ever performed. Scripture indicated that it occurred on the third day. Jesus was also resurrected from the dead on the third day.

Third-day miracles require more perseverance than instantaneous miracles. Let's be honest; we love a good story where God shows up immediately. While this makes for a good story, this is not always the case. Mary and Martha waited four days before Jesus showed up. Daniel prayed and waited 21 days for his response. Some miracles just take time.

How many of us miss out on our miracles because we give up after the first day? What are you believing Jesus for today? Today is a good day for a miracle!

231

GUARDRAILS ARE THERE TO PROTECT YOU

Don't cheat your neighbor by moving the ancient boundary markers set up by previous generations.
Proverbs 22:28

Boundary stones served to distinguish one person's property from another person's property. Essentially, it is the chain-link fence that separates your property from your neighbor's property. Boundary stones also served to indicate you were leaving protected property and entering property owned by an enemy.

Boundaries serve as guides to show us where the line is in our lives. What one generation allows in moderation, the next generation will take to excess. My wife and I don't drink, not because we are pastors, but because we have personally seen the destructive effects it has had on many of our family members. We also understand that we have to model self-control to our children. When someone drinks too much, there is a loss of self-control. If you don't draw the line for your children, they won't know where to stop.

THE GOOD, THE BAD, AND THE UGLY!

But one day when Saul was sitting at home, with spear in hand, the tormenting spirit from the LORD suddenly came upon him again. As David played his harp, Saul hurled his spear at David. But David dodged out of the way, and leaving the spear stuck in the wall, he fled and escaped into the night.
1 Samuel 19:9-10

The writer of 1 Samuel, clearly indicates that Saul was not the best leader. It makes no effort to paint him in a good light. The great part about the Scriptures is that they always include the good, the bad, and the ugly. The Bible is definitely not a G-rated book! More often than not, we learn more about what not to do rather than what we should do. Many of the most notable characters of the Bible had some major character issues.

For some reason, God saw fit for David to serve King Saul for a few years of his life. This was a tough season for David, especially beings Saul tried to pin him to the wall with a spear on more than one occasion. Despite all of this, God had a reason for allowing David to have this experience. Sometimes, God will allow you to serve a Saul so you will learn what not to do when it's your turn to lead. Remember, pain has a long memory.

233

DON'T BE DEAF

God detests the prayers of a person who ignores the law.
Proverbs 28:9

God is not a slot machine. We can't put in a few coins, pull the handle, and expect our blessings to come out. It doesn't work that way. He's not looking for a one-sided relationship. He's looking for intimacy and for someone who has an open ear to listen to His instructions. As a parent of two teenagers and two young children, I am always looking for ways to bless them. Still, I also understand that I cannot bless disobedience, especially when they do something I have already told them not to do. Likewise, if you ignore God's Word, He'll ignore your words!

DON'T SKIP THE PROCESS

So he took Joseph and threw him into the prison where the king's
prisoners were held, and there he remained.
Genesis 39:20

Joseph's life was a series of setups, setbacks, and promotions. When he was 17 years old, he dreamed of his parents and brothers bowing down before him. In his dream, he saw himself in a high leadership position. He was destined for greatness, but it was a road paved with pain.

Joseph didn't start out in Pharaoh's palace. He went from the pit to Potiphar's house to Pharaoh's prison to Pharaoh's palace. He certainly busted the myth of the overnight success. His Instagram picture montage wouldn't have exactly been someone you would want to follow. Doing the dishes or sitting behind bars isn't exactly the influencer life for which he had hoped.

Too many people want to jump from Potiphar's house to Pharaoh's palace without going to Pharaoh's prison. God is just as interested in the process as He is in the destination. The prison prepares you for the pressures of the palace. If you're in the prison today, you're in a good place. It's the place of in-between. You are in between what's good and what's best. Keep dreaming and keep doing the dishes!

GOD IS THINKING ABOUT YOU!

How precious are your thoughts about me, O God. They cannot be numbered! I can't even count them; they outnumber the grains of sand! And when I wake up, you are still with me!
Psalm 139:17-18

My family and I have just returned from vacation at the beach. We love going to the beach. It's hard to go wrong with sun, sand, and water. Have you ever tried counting sand? It's impossible, and yet, that's how much God thinks about you!

Parents, do you ever just smile at your children and think how much you love them and how proud you are of them? Do you know that God feels the same about you? You are the apple of His eye, and His thoughts towards you outnumber the grains of sand!

OPEN DOORS

Giving a gift can open doors; it gives access to important people!
Proverbs 18:16

People love being around generous people. There are many takers in the world but few givers. The givers always find a way to stand out among the crowd. If you need a door opened in your life, don't be afraid to give. Generosity opens doors in your life!

IT JUST MIGHT TAKE A WHILE

The Israelite territory now extended all the way from Mount Halak, which leads up to Seir in the south, as far north as Baal-gad at the foot of Mount Hermon in the valley of Lebanon. Joshua killed all the kings of those territories, waging war for a long time to accomplish this.
Joshua 11:17-18

Few things in life happen overnight. Joshua and the Israelites were given the Promised Land, but it didn't come to them all at once. They had to go out and fight for it. The fighting lasted a few years, not a few days! It just might take a while to see the results you're wanting to see. Anything in your life worth having is going to require a battle. The longer the battle, the greater the reward! Fight on!

238

THE WORD OF GOD ENDURES

The grass withers and the flowers fade, but the word of our God stands
forever.
Isaiah 40:8

The Word of God never changes. It doesn't change with the different seasons of life. It's the one constant in your life that you can count on. It's not subject to the economy or who is in the White House. God's Word does not have term limits. It does not have a start and end date. God's Word doesn't have a shelf life. His promises never have an expiration date, so keep praying and believing!

THE TRUTH HURTS

Wounds from a sincere friend are better than many kisses from an enemy.
Proverbs 27:6

A few years ago, I had an authority figure in my life correct me. Truth be told, his words cut me. As I complained about (prayed about) what he said, the Holy Spirit reminded me of this verse. I had to take a step back and realize that this person corrected me, because he saw potential in me. If someone corrects you, it's because they believe in your potential. Sometimes the truth hurts.

I would also caution you; there is a difference between criticism and correction. The difference between the two is the intention. If a friend or mentor corrects you, it's because he or she wants to see you grow. If someone criticizes you, it's usually out of jealousy, envy, bitterness, or unresolved pain. A good rule of thumb: never take criticism from someone you wouldn't take advice from.

240

THE SECRET PLACE

But when you pray, go away by yourself, shut the door behind you, and
pray to your Father in private. Then your Father, who sees everything,
will reward you.
Matthew 6:6

Over the years, I've had many students ask how they can get the anointing on their lives. My answer is always twofold: You have to spend a lot of time in the secret place, and you have to go through some stuff and live to talk about it.

God likes to reward what is done in secret in your life. Even when others do not see your sacrifice, God always does. When you do something without the need for a pat on the back or for the accolades, it's incredible what the Lord can do in and through you. He'll also reward you for your efforts.

241

WHAT ARE YOU LEANING ON?

Trust in the LORD with all your heart; do not depend on your own understanding. Seek his will in all you do, and he will show you which path to take.

Proverbs 3:5-6

For most of his life, Jacob relied on his own ingenuity and his own understanding to make things happen for himself. He was known as a deceiver and a conniver when he stole his brother's birthright. After many years of doing his own thing and leaning on himself, it all finally came to a head. When he had nothing left, he wrestled with God until daybreak (Gen. 32:22-32). At the end of this wrestling match, he begged God for a blessing, and surprisingly God touched him, but He dislocated his hip in the process. Jacob walked with a limp for the rest of his life and had to lean upon a staff. It was a gentle reminder that he had to rely upon God and his strength. The writer of Hebrews describes the end of Jacob's life this way, "It was by faith that Jacob, when he was old and dying, blessed each of Joseph's sons and bowed in worship as he leaned on his staff" (Heb. 11:21). At the end of his life, he was leaning, but he was worshipping. What you rely on will reveal where you put your trust. What are you leaning on?

242

ADD TO YOUR LEARNING

Instruct the wise, and they will be even wiser. Teach the righteous, and they will learn even more.
Proverbs 9:9

Several years ago, I was interested in learning more about blogging and writing. In the process, I discovered a successful blogger who lived in the Atlanta area. After I spent a good deal of time reading everything he had written, I finally mustered the courage to email him. I offered to drive to him and buy him breakfast. Surprisingly, he responded and said he would be glad to meet with me. I came prepared for our meeting with a page full of questions. I didn't eat much that morning because I wanted to ask all my questions and honor his time. At the end of our time together, I asked him why he said yes to a complete stranger. He said, "Well, I normally charge $500 an hour for consulting like this, but you asked, and you made it convenient for me. I have to eat breakfast and who doesn't like a free meal? Besides, I like to help people when I can."

That hour of free advice cost me less than $20 and two hours of driving. It's much cheaper to learn from the mistakes of others than to pay the full price yourself.

DON'T CRY OVER DRIED UP BROOKS

But after a while the brook dried up, for there was no rainfall anywhere in the land.

1 Kings 17:7

For a short season, Elijah the Prophet had it made. Every morning and evening the ravens brought him bread and meat and he drank from the brook (1 Kings 17:5-6). That's not a bad gig. Like clockwork, God sent his food via Door Dash. It showed up every morning and every evening. While this was great while it lasted, nothing lasts forever.

To help nudge him toward his next season of ministry, the Lord caused the brook to dry up. God will often use discomfort to push us in the direction of our purpose. God instructed him to go to Zarephath, where a widow would feed him. One small problem: the Lord didn't tell the widow that Elijah was coming.

In many cases, before God can start something new in your life, He has to stop something old. Sometimes when a brook dries up, He's redirecting you to something else. A brook is a temporary provision for a temporary need. Don't cry over a dried-up brook when God is asking you to move on to something else. Your new provision won't come until you step out and move on from your dried-up brook.

244

DON'T BE AFRAID OF SECLUSION

When Zechariah's week of service in the Temple was over, he returned home.
Soon afterward his wife, Elizabeth, became pregnant and went into seclusion
for five months.
Luke 1:23-24

In our culture of constant notifications and pings of our phones, we rarely have time to disconnect or be alone. We are addicted to the adrenaline rush of distractions and being wanted. We can rarely hear from God because of all the noise going on around us. There are times in our lives where we need to step away from the normal and from the daily grind and allow God to speak to us and to do some things in our lives.

Seclusion is not a bad thing if it causes you to grow closer to the Lord. In the case of Elizabeth, she became pregnant and went into seclusion so that what was in her life had time to grow and to give birth to the dream God had placed in her. Sometimes the Lord keeps you in seclusion to birth some new things in your life. If you're feeling secluded today, it could be that the Lord wants to birth something new in your life. Seclusion is only wasted when you fail to embrace the intimacy it creates.

BE THE KING'S FRIEND

Ahithophel was the royal adviser. Hushai the Arkite was the king's friend.
1 Chronicles 27:33

This chapter of 1 Chronicles reads like a who's who list of impressive people. It doesn't mean anything to us today, but at that time, the list represented the best and most talented leaders. It included the best military commanders, leaders of the tribes, and officials of David's kingdom. It's quite an impressive list.

In this list, one person stands out among the rest. His resume doesn't seem very impressive. We don't know that much about him, but we know he was the king's friend. Hushai the Arkite was the king's friend. Imagine if that was your only job. His only job was to spend time with the king and be his friend. In the New Testament, Jesus speaks of His disciples saying, "I no longer call you slaves, because a master doesn't confide in his slaves. Now you are my friends, since I have told you everything the Father told me" (John 15:15).

Being the King's friend is the only job you need. Would He call you His friend today? If not, He's just waiting on you to spend time with Him.

246

DON'T BE FOOLISH

As dead flies cause even a bottle of perfume to stink, so a little foolishness spoils great wisdom and honor.
Ecclesiastes 10:1

Unfortunately, people remember our follies and our mistakes more than our good deeds. When it comes to remembering what you've done for them, people have short memories. When it comes to remembering something you've done to them, people have long memories. Memories are fickle like that.

With this in mind, it is good to remember that reputations are easier to maintain than to restore. It takes a lifetime to build a good reputation, but it can be lost in a moment. As believers, we must live our lives above reproach and avoid the appearance of evil (1 Thess. 5:22).

247

DON'T GIVE UP

So let's not get tired of doing what is good. At just the right time we will reap a harvest of blessing if we don't give up.
Galatians 6:9

Let's face it. Everyone gets tired at some point in life. It's especially tough when you're tired because you've been doing your best to do the right thing. It's easy to give up when you do not see the end in sight or when you're not seeing any progress. In this verse, the Apostle Paul reminds us there is a proper time for a harvest. In the natural realm, we all understand when you plant a seed in the ground, it's not going to immediately shoot up in front of you. It's going to take a few days or even a few weeks.

Bamboo is a robust and resilient plant, but it takes three years before you'll see anything come out of the ground. Likewise, in the kingdom of God, you will face seasons when you don't see anything happening. Still, you must trust the Holy Spirit is at work below the surface of things. When the time is right, you'll see a harvest. The key is not to give up or dig up your seed.

248

MOVING ON!

After Lot had gone, the LORD said to Abram, "Look as far as you can see in every direction—north and south, east and west. I am giving all this land, as far as you can see, to you and your descendants as a permanent possession. And I will give you so many descendants that, like the dust of the earth, they cannot be counted! Go and walk through the land in every direction, for I am giving it to you."
Genesis 13:14-17

When Abraham first heard the command of God to leave his homeland and his family and travel to a new Promised Land, he took his nephew, Lot, with him. We don't know why he included Lot, but maybe it was because Abraham didn't have any offspring, or because Lot's father had died.

Interestingly, God did not speak directly to Abraham again until after he separated from Lot. It was only after they parted ways that God appeared to him again and confirmed the promise. Abraham never received his Isaac until he separated himself from Lot.

Some people in your current circle can't go to where God is wanting to take you. It's going to require you to let go of some friendships that are holding you back.

QUIT MAKING EXCUSES!

Farmers who wait for perfect weather never plant. If they watch every cloud, they never harvest.
Ecclesiastes 11:4

You'll either find an excuse, or you'll find a way. If you wait for the perfect situation or perfect circumstances, you'll never step out in faith. There will always be an element of risk involved with faith. The dictionary is the only place where reward comes before risk.

God can't bless what you don't start. What has God asked you to start? God is not asking you to jump; He's only asking you to take a step of faith. You should use wisdom, but be careful not to fall prey to paralysis by analysis. Don't wait on perfect circumstances or let fear hold you back. Get started now!

250

I KNOW WHERE YOU STAY!

"But I know you well—where you stay and when you come and go. I know the
way you have raged against me. And because of your raging against me and
your arrogance, which I have heard for myself, I will put my hook in your nose
and my bit in your mouth. I will make you return by the same road on which
you came."
Isaiah 37:28-29

In this chapter Sennacherib the king of Assyria, was threatening to attack
Israel. He sent a letter to King Hezekiah of Israel with threats of destruction. In response to the letter, King Hezekiah did the only thing he knew
to do. He went to the temple of the Lord and spread out the letter before
the Lord in prayer. God likes it when prayer is our first response, not our
last resort.

These are excellent verses, as the Lord talks to the enemies of Israel.
He reminds them that He knows where they stay and when they come
and go. Nothing escapes God's attention in your life.

Early the next morning, the angel of the LORD went out and put to
death 185,000 in the Assyrian camp. I love it when God gets mad at our
enemies and says, "I know where you stay!"

GOD HEARS, AND GOD RESPONDS!

He will listen to the prayers of the destitute. He will not reject their pleas.
Psalm 102:17

Your prayers to God do not go in one ear and out the other. Not only does God hear your prayers, but He also responds to your prayers. He's not too busy or too distracted to hear your voice. In fact, He longs to hear your voice. When you're desperate for God, you have His full attention.

Being desperate for Him is a good place to be because you have His full attention. You never have God's attention more than when you're hurting or in need. Don't believe the lies of the enemy. God doesn't despise your requests; He longs to hear you ask Him.

CONTAGIOUS COURAGE

In another battle with the Philistines at Gath, they encountered a huge man with six fingers on each hand and six toes on each foot, twenty-four in all, who was also a descendant of the giants.
2 Samuel 21:20

Jonathan was David's nephew. Evidently, he heard the story of David killing Goliath when he was a young man. He might have even had a life-size poster of David triumphantly standing over the giant in his bedroom. Indeed, he heard all the stories of David's victories. He likely grew up with his own dreams of one day killing a giant. Courage is contagious.

Someone in your future is going to need to see your courage. Someone just needs to know it can be done! Your courage today will be someone's deliverance tomorrow.

WORKING BEFORE KINGS

Do you see any truly competent workers? They will serve kings rather than working for ordinary people.
Proverbs 22:29

Never put yourself in a position where you must choose between skill and character. Education is not just about knowledge; it's about who you become in the process. Skill will place you before kings; your character will keep you there.

254

FINISH STRONG!

*He will keep you strong to the end so that you will be free from all
blame on the day when our Lord Jesus Christ returns.*
1 Corinthians 1:8

Being a Christian is not just about having fire insurance. The goal of a
follower of Jesus is not simply to safely arrive in heaven. The goal is to
finish strong and to do all you can with what you can.

My goal as a believer is to stand before the Lord without blame and to
hear the words, "Well done, my good and faithful servant" (Matthew
25:23).

255

PLOWING YOUR FIELDS

So Elijah went and found Elisha son of Shaphat plowing a field. There were twelve teams of oxen in the field, and Elisha was plowing with the twelfth team. Elijah went over to him and threw his cloak across his shoulders and then walked away.

1 Kings 19:19

God anoints hard work. Elisha was doing the work of a servant. He had twelve teams of oxen, which is a good indicator that business was going well. He had a large enough field for twelve teams of oxen to be plowing, and he was plowing with the twelfth team. He wasn't afraid to get his hands dirty. When Elijah found him, Elisha was working.

The anointing is never an excuse for laziness. God is looking to anoint people who aren't afraid to work. Don't wait until you're noticed before you decide to put in the work. If you want God's attention, don't be afraid to do what might be considered beneath you.

DON'T GET BORED

In the spring of the year, when kings normally go out to war, David sent Joab and the Israelite army to fight the Ammonites. They destroyed the Ammonite army and laid siege to the city of Rabbah. However, David stayed behind in Jerusalem.

2 Samuel 11:1

David remained in Jerusalem because he was comfortable. Things were going well. His stock portfolio was up, he was acquiring new rental properties, and everything seemed to be going his way. Things were going so well he sent his army out to fight because he had convinced himself that he could delegate this part of his job. If you read the rest of these verses, you will remember this is where he saw Bathsheba bathing and coveted her so much that he had her brought to him for a one-night stand. In the end, she became pregnant, David had her righteous husband killed in battle, and David was an adulterer.

Bored people sin. The most dangerous time in a person's life is when he or she is not fighting a battle. The desire for comfort is a subtle enemy; it causes us to slumber when there's more territory to be conquered. Keep fighting!

DON'T WORRY ABOUT IT!

"That is why I tell you not to worry about everyday life—whether you have enough food and drink, or enough clothes to wear. Isn't life more than food, and your body more than clothing?"
Matthew 6:25

Worrying is paying a deposit on a problem you don't have. Worrying never solves problems and can never provide solutions. It can only make you miserable and drag you down.

You can worry or you can worship, but you can't do both. They're both a choice, so choose wisely!

YOU ARE AN HEIR

And since we are his children, we are his heirs. In fact, together with Christ we are heirs of God's glory. But if we are to share his glory, we must also share his suffering.

Romans 8:17

I recently read the story of a homeless man in Arizona. This man lived on the streets, and day after day, he resorted to begging for food and trying to find shelter every night. Come to find out, a family member had left the man a sizable inheritance, but he lived totally unaware of what was available to him.

Too many Christians are like the homeless man. He didn't know it, but he had an inheritance waiting for him, and all he had to do was claim it. As Christians, many of us are this way. We walk around as spiritual vagrants, and we don't realize the inheritance we've been given. We are joint heirs with Jesus Christ, and He is a friend that sticks closer than a brother!

LET HONESTY BE YOUR GUIDE

Honesty guides good people; dishonesty destroys treacherous people.
Proverbs 11:3

I was reading about the Great Wall of China. It's so large you can see it from space! The Chinese built this magnificent structure to withstand invading armies. While focusing on the strength of the structure, the emperors neglected one thing. They neglected the building of the character of the gatekeepers. On countless occasions, invaders bribed the gatekeepers to get inside. More invaders entered through bribing the gatekeepers than through breaking through the wall. This is a great lesson for us today. Their greatest threat came from the enemy on the inside, not the outside. We need to develop integrity, as it will protect us. Without integrity, we are open to destruction.

260

SHAKE IT OFF!

But Paul shook off the snake into the fire and was unharmed.
Acts 28:5

The last few weeks had been rough. Paul had been on a boat headed for Rome, and it had taken longer than expected to get there. At every turn, they seemed to encounter another storm. In this passage, they encountered a storm and ended up being shipwrecked on the Island of Malta. After going ashore, they all started gathering wood to make a fire to dry off and keep warm. Paul was doing the right thing, but he got bitten by a snake. Scripture says the snake "was driven out by the heat." Has this ever happened to you? Have you ever tried to do the right thing and ended up snake-bitten? I suspect all of us can relate to this story in some way or another. Anytime we attempt something for God, we put heat on the enemy. He hates the heat caused by righteous people. One of his greatest tactics is to discourage people from doing the right thing.

Paul was snake-bitten, but he didn't suffer the effects of the bite. Scripture says, "No weapon turned against you will succeed" (Isaiah 54:17). It never says the weapon won't be formed; however, it does say it won't prevail over us. Just shake it off!

THE LORD IS WITH YOU

"For the L<small>ORD</small> *your God is going with you! He will fight for you against your enemies, and he will give you victory!"*
Deuteronomy 20:4

Winston Churchill once said, "If you're going through hell, keep going." This came from a man who led the nation of Great Britain during a time of national crisis. They were knee-deep in a war with Hitler while facing impossible odds. He knew something about obtaining victory. I don't know if Churchill was a Christian, but he understood the principle of perseverance: you'll walk in victory if you simply refuse to give up.

Early in my Christian walk, I would get upset at the Lord when I found myself in a crisis. For some reason, I thought the Lord would protect me from everything and that life was supposed to be trouble-free. The more I matured and read the Word, the more I realized that God does not guarantee a trouble-free life but rather a life filled with the presence of God. Jesus said, "In this life you will have trouble, but don't worry I have overcome the world."

Just because the Lord assures you of victory, doesn't mean you won't have to fight for it. If you're fighting for something today, know the Lord is with you in the fight, and the two of you are the majority.

262

IT'S OKAY TO BE HARDHEADED!

As the time drew near for him to ascend to heaven, Jesus resolutely set out for
Jerusalem.
Luke 9:51

Growing up, my father would say, "Boy, you're hardheaded!" He said this because whenever I got an idea in my head, I would just do it without regard for the consequences. When my mind was made up about something, you couldn't tell me otherwise.

Jesus had hardheaded faith and determination as well. Luke 9:51 says, "As the time drew near for him to ascend to heaven, Jesus resolutely set out for Jerusalem."

In this verse, we see a glimpse of Jesus' determination and tenacity. Jesus knew that death awaited Him in Jerusalem. In the Greek text, the word "resolutely" means to "set one's face like flint." In other words, Jesus made up His mind; He would do the will of the Father regardless of His own personal comfort. Jesus came to set the captives free. Jesus did not have a Plan B. He was determined to be obedient. It was all or nothing.

FOLLOWING AT A DISTANCE

So they arrested him and led him to the high priest's home. And Peter followed
at a distance.
Luke 22:54

I used to drive in Atlanta traffic every day, and it could be vicious at times. Years later, when my wife was riding with me, she made the candid observation: "You're following too close!"

Many of us want to be close to Christ. We pray, read our Bible, and attend church once a week—or twice a week if we really mean business. All too often, however, we are afraid to "follow too close" because deep down, we think it will cost us something.

I think the Apostle Peter thought this as well. After Jesus was arrested, he understood it might cost him his life if he got too close. We often choose to "follow at a distance" as Peter did. The night before Jesus' arrest, Peter stood up and swore he would never leave Christ's side. He would die with Him if he had to, but when the time came, Peter followed from a "safe distance."

Peter knew that if he followed too close, those who arrested Jesus could also arrest him. Peter wasn't willing to pay the same price as Jesus. Later, Peter would disown Jesus three times. Immediately, Peter realized what he had done, and he wept bitterly. Jesus, with all the love He had for Peter, forgave him. In fact, when Jesus was raised from the dead, He told the women at the tomb to "go tell Peter and the other disciples that I have risen." Jesus forgave Peter and restored him. Later, Peter would preach a powerful sermon on the Day of Pentecost and watch over 3,000 people get saved! Peter would become one of the most outstanding leaders of the Early Church.

What made the difference in Peter's life? I think Peter realized the depth of Christ's love for him. He saw Christ die on the cross for him. He also saw that when Christ rose from the dead, Jesus sought him out. Like Peter, Christ seeks us out every day. He yearns for us to come close. He invites us to be in His presence. He wants us to follow close and not from a safe distance. It will cost us something to follow close, but it will be worth it!

BETWEEN A ROCK AND A HARD PLACE

On the day of the attack, David said to his troops, "I hate those 'lame' and 'blind' Jebusites. Whoever attacks them should strike by going into the city through the water tunnel." That is the origin of the saying, "The blind and the lame may not enter the house."
2 Samuel 5:8

Webster's Dictionary defines the phrase "between a rock and a hard place" "as being in a difficult or uncomfortable position with no attractive way out." Have you ever been forced to go through a rock and a hard place? I have on several occasions in my life. I went through the loss of a parent during my last semester of college. I had to live in my mother-in-law's garage for six years while I worked full-time and completed school. A few years ago, I endured a company layoff and had to take a significant pay cut. I could keep going, but I don't want to depress you. The point I'm making is that everyone eventually faces a between a rock and a hard place experience.

In the Old Testament, King David found himself in a difficult position. David and his men marched to Jerusalem to attack the enemy. In verse 8, David told his men they would have to use the water shaft to capture the city. This water shaft was located at the northern end of the

Pool of Siloam, which helps provide Jerusalem's water supply. The waterway was an arched passageway that started out considerably large but gradually narrowed down to a diameter of 14 inches. It's hard to imagine grown men crawling through a 14-inch water shaft to get into the city of Jerusalem. Scholars say it would have taken about four hours to crawl through this passageway. By the time they got through this rough spot, they were bruised, cut, and bleeding. You might be bleeding and have some scars, but you've made it. A scar is just a reminder that you've been through some stuff. Even Jesus has scars. It puts us in good company!

ESCAPE THE CAVE

So David left Gath and escaped to the cave of Adullam. Soon his brothers and all his other relatives joined him there. Then others began coming—men who were in trouble or in debt or who were just discontented—until David was the captain of about 400 men.
1 Samuel 22:1-2

Have you ever hit rock bottom in your life? Does it seem like no matter how hard you try, nothing is going right for you? You're good to your neighbors, you tithe, give to missions, and teach Sunday School—but still, nothing is going right. During these times, it's easy to find yourself in a cave of despair. If you're in a cave right now, take heart because you aren't the first one to end up there.

In 1 Samuel 22:1-5, David found himself in the cave of Adullam. This was probably the lowest point in his life. Some scholars believe Adullam means "place of no foreseeable future."

If you're in a cave today, you must get to a place where you can hear God's Word. David had sunk so low that God had to send a prophet to coax him out of the cave: "One day the prophet Gad told David, 'Leave the stronghold and return to the land of Judah.' So David went to the forest of Hereth" (1 Samuel 22:5).

Judah means praise. The prophet Gad was telling David to go live in Judah. Sometimes you have to praise your way out of your darkness! One of the best ways to recharge your faith is to thank and praise God for what He's done in your past. When you praise God for His deliverance in the past, it gives you hope for your future.

266

JUST KEEP WALKING

After sending them home, he went up into the hills by himself to pray. Night fell while he was there alone.
Matthew 14:23

Every time Jesus faced a crisis, He prayed. In this passage, Jesus spent time praying before He went and faced the storm. Prayer wasn't Jesus' last resort; it was His first option.

Jesus also understood that action squelches fear every time. Jesus didn't sit down in the middle of the storm. He kept walking. When storms are circling around you, it's no time to sit down, cry, and hope for the best. It's time to keep moving and doing what you would typically do. If Jesus had let fear control Him, He wouldn't have been able to get to where His Father wanted Him to be. Your Father has a plan and purpose for your life. Don't be afraid to fight for it.

DON'T SETTLE FOR SECOND PLACE

I don't mean to say that I have already achieved these things or that I have already reached perfection. But I press on to possess that perfection for which Christ Jesus first possessed me. No, dear brothers and sisters, I have not achieved it, but I focus on this one thing: Forgetting the past and looking forward to what lies ahead, I press on to reach the end of the race and receive the heavenly prize for which God, through Christ Jesus, is calling us.
Philippians 3:12-14

Several years ago, I was watching the Daytona 500. As I was watched the race wind down, the cameras were focused on Jeff Gordon. He had been in second place for most of the race and had not attempted to get to the first position. It almost seemed as if he was happy running second. Even the announcers seemed perplexed by his inaction. They made a few comments questioning why Jeff hadn't made a move—when he had the ability to do so.

About six laps from the final lap, the owner of Jeff Gordon's car came over the radio and asked, "When are you going to make your move? We didn't come here to run second!"

When I heard this, I thought to myself, "That's a pretty profound question to ask!"

Rick Hendrick didn't want to settle for second because he understood the payout for the race. He also understood the importance of the race because he had a long view of the season ahead. Over the years, he learned that every victory during the season brought him one step closer to the big prize. Championships aren't won in a single race or game but over a season of victories.

I couldn't help but wonder: "How many of us have settled for second place in our lives?" Where in your life have you settled for second? What little change in your life could you make that would make the biggest impact? What dream have you given up on that God has not?

LAYING IT DOWN

Then, calling the crowd to join his disciples, he said, "If any of you wants to be my follower, you must give up your own way, take up your cross, and follow me. If you try to hang on to your life, you will lose it. But if you give up your life for my sake and for the sake of the Good News, you will save it."
Mark 8:34-35

Have you ever tried picking up too many things at once? What happened when you tried this? Most of the time, we drop everything we were attempting to carry.

In order to take up your cross and follow Jesus, you have to lay some things down first. It's hard to carry a cross if your hands are already full.

Many believers are attempting to carry things the Lord never asked them to carry. Are your hands full of bad habits, negative thought patterns, past pains, or failures? Are you holding unforgiveness in your heart? What do you need to lay down in order to pick up and carry your cross?

THE BLESSING OF HARDSHIP

But the more the Egyptians oppressed them, the more the Israelites multiplied and spread, and the more alarmed the Egyptians became. So the Egyptians worked the people of Israel without mercy.
Exodus 1:12-13

The Egyptians grew increasingly afraid of the Israelites, so they began to persecute them ruthlessly. They thought that by persecuting them, the Israelites would stop increasing. However, it seemed to have a reverse effect because the more they oppressed the Israelites, the more they grew. Satan still uses this tactic with God's people.

Lesson to be learned: persecution produces multiplication in your life. Around the world, Christians are being persecuted, and the Church is still spreading. God often uses persecution to multiply His people.

On a personal level, the best growth in your walk with God comes when you are facing hardship. You may not realize it at the time, but you can look back and see how far God has brought you. If God is allowing you to experience difficulty, rest assured, He wants to produce something of significance in your life.

Today's hardship becomes your training ground for your Promised Land!

270

WORK IS A BLESSING

The LORD will guarantee a blessing on everything you do and will fill your storehouses with grain. The LORD your God will bless you in the land he is giving you.
Deuteronomy 28:8

In the Old Testament, the Lord promises to bless the work of our hands. In many modern churches, we've taught people to pray and expect God's blessing in our lives. While this is true, God's blessing most often comes in the form of more work. Thomas Edison once said, "Opportunity is missed by most people because it comes dressed in overalls and looks like work."

The Lord expects us to do our part as well. The Lord won't bless what we aren't doing. Why would the Lord bless our business or ministry if we aren't doing anything? He usually blesses us as we are doing something or after we've done our part. He doesn't bless before because it would remove the element of faith in our lives. If you're not doing something, the key is to start somewhere.

THE COST OF FREE SAMPLES

So the Israelites examined their food, but they did not consult the LORD.
Joshua 9:14

I don't know anyone who doesn't like free samples. If you've ever been to Sam's Club on a Saturday afternoon, you know what I'm talking about. You could go in there and feed your entire family on samples!

Samples are intentionally enticing. Marketers instinctively know that if they can get you to try something once and have a good experience, the likelihood of you purchasing more is much greater than it would have been if you had never tried it.

In Joshua 9:1-27, the Israelites made a treaty with the Gibeonites. The Lord had explicitly warned the Israelites to not make any treaties or compromises with the people of Canaan. It all started when they didn't recognize their enemy standing in front of them. The enemy came dressed in a disguise and allowed Joshua and his men to sample their provisions.

I've learned that big sins have small beginnings, and their roots are always grounded in compromise. Whatever you do, don't compromise your standards!

THE MAKING OF A CHAMPION (PART 1)

These are the names of David's mightiest warriors. The first was Jashobeam the Hacmonite, who was leader of the Three—the three mightiest warriors among David's men. He once used his spear to kill 800 enemy warriors in a single battle.
2 Samuel 23:8

This chapter recounts David's last words. This is the story of David and his Mighty Men. These were the same characters who were in the cave of Adullam (1 Samuel 22). Now they are champions. This group of men went from being a group of zeros to a group of heroes. These guys were the Navy Seals of David's day. These were some bad dudes!

Josheb was significantly outnumbered, and he still defeated 800 men! Champions don't worry about their age, inexperience, or talents. Champions realize it's not about them.

A few years ago, I was called to visit a young lady in the hospital. I had never met the lady; I only knew her aunt and uncle who attended our church. When I arrived, the doctor had just called the family in to say goodbye because her kidneys and liver were shutting down. I walked into a dying woman's room and didn't know what was going on. As I walked into the ICU waiting room, her family wasn't taking it very well. Some of them were weeping hysterically. I didn't know what to do but pray. It's amazing what you'll do when you don't have options.

Before I started praying, I looked at her family and shouted, "She's not dead yet!" This was an obvious statement, but I wanted to help them muster some faith before we prayed. A couple of family members looked at me and said, "You're right. She's not dead yet."

It didn't look good, but we began to pray and called other people to pray with us. She didn't die that day or the next day. Slowly things began to turn around. It didn't happen immediately, but a couple of days later, she was in a regular room, sitting up, talking, and eating. A champion has courage in the face of impossible odds (2 Samuel 23:8).

THE MAKING OF A CHAMPION (PART 2)

He killed Philistines until his hand was too tired to lift his sword, and the LORD
gave him a great victory that day. The rest of the army did not return until it
was time to collect the plunder!
2 Samuel 23:10

A champion has courage in the face of indescribable fatigue. His body grew tired from fighting, but he wouldn't let go of his sword. Sometimes a champion will get tired from fighting, but he must continue to swing his sword. When everyone else drops the sword and runs, you must stick to it. Many Christians are trying to fight the battle without their sword.

A few years ago, my youngest daughter was bitten on the arm by an ant. She was scared of the minuscule ant because it had bitten her. Even though she was much bigger than the ant and had much more power, she was afraid of the ant. I told her to smash the ant the next time she saw one. I even demonstrated it for her.

She didn't realize the power available to her because she didn't apply it to her life! As believers, many of us operate like my daughter. We never use the power that is available to us. Instead, we let the enemy keep biting us. Learn to swing your sword!

THE MAKING OF A CHAMPION (PART 3)

but Shammah held his ground in the middle of the field and beat back the
Philistines. So the LORD *brought about a great victory.*
2 Samuel 23:12

The men of Israel retreated. While they fled, Shammah took a stand. Everyone around him retreated, but he was a champion, and he wouldn't give up his ground to the enemy.

Many people give up when life gets too difficult. Too many prayers go unanswered because someone gives up too soon or quits. It's easy to buy into the brand of Christianity that says everything should come easy and without a struggle. Anything of value in life is going to require a struggle. If it's worth having, it's worth the struggle. Some things in your life are worth fighting for!

275

THINK BEFORE YOU SPEAK

The tongue of the wise makes knowledge appealing, but the mouth of a fool belches out foolishness.
Proverbs 15:2

Learn to think before you speak. In a crowd, the fool usually speaks first. You cannot listen if you're too busy talking.

Sometimes you need to take a moment and ask yourself, "How are they going to receive what I am about to say? How could they perceive this?" Most arguments can be avoided if you'll stop to think before you speak. Today's takeaway: Don't be a fool!

DON'T BE A DREAM KILLER

It is foolish to belittle one's neighbor; a sensible person keeps quiet.
Proverbs 11:12

The word "belittle" means "to speak slightingly of." It means to degrade someone and to put them down.

It's easy to be negative and to be a dream killer. It doesn't take much to find something to complain about or to kill someone's dreams. It takes more energy to hold your tongue and to be a positive person.

BE A TRUTH-TELLER

Gentle words are a tree of life; a deceitful tongue crushes the spirit.
Proverbs 15:4

It takes a lifetime to build trust, but trust can be lost in a moment. Lying to a person is the easiest way to destroy a relationship. It usually takes a long time and a lot effort to earn someone's trust back. The best thing to do is not to lie in the first place.

We have a choice to make: will we use our tongues to bring life or to bring death? What's your choice going to be?

278

LEARN TO SHUT UP!

Watch your tongue and keep your mouth shut, and you will stay out of trouble.
Proverbs 21:23

You don't have to get the last word. (It pained me to type that!) If you want to keep calamity out of your house, you need to learn to be quiet. This is certainly easier said than done, especially if you have to win every argument. You can win every argument and still lose, especially if you destroy someone in the process. Sometimes it's better to overlook an offense.

279

DON'T NAG PEOPLE!

Too much talk leads to sin. Be sensible and keep your mouth shut.
Proverbs 10:19

Most people resent being nagged. Nagging requires continual fault-finding in a person and then endlessly urging them to do something about their faults. Rarely does nagging someone work for long. Guilt doesn't motivate people for very long either.

As a parent of teenagers, I am having to learn this. I want to urge them to do something, but if I'm not careful, my urging bleeds over into nagging. It's better to say something once and then let it go.

PATIENCE CAN BREAK A BONE

Patience can persuade a prince, and soft speech can break bones.
Proverbs 25:15

If you want to change someone's mind about something, try being gentler with your words. I told my wife the other day, "Be patient with me because the Lord is still working on me." In return, she said, "I know He is, but He's using me to help you!"

If you will be patient with others and talk to them the right way, you can usually change their mind on something. My wife is the queen of this skill. I have often found myself going somewhere while asking, "How in the world did I get talked into this?" It's always because my wife has learned to respond with grace.

AVOID MOCKERY!

Throw out the mocker, and fighting goes, too. Quarrels and insults will disappear.
Proverbs 22:10

To mock someone means to ridicule them. Some of us were raised in homes where we constantly mocked one another. When you get married, you do not marry your sister or your brother. If you want to get rid of strife and quarrels in your marriage, quit tearing each other down.

Look for ways to compliment your spouse. What are they good at? What do they do well? If your husband is a good provider, then tell him he is. If your wife is a good cook, then tell her she is. If she's not a good cook, speak it by faith!

You might be thinking your relationship is too far gone, but I would encourage you to ask the Holy Spirit to help you. Ask the Holy Spirit to change you. Ask Him to help you to use your words to bring life to those around you.

UPPER ROOM CHRISTIANS

During this time, when about 120 believers were together in one place,
Peter stood up and addressed them.

Acts 1:15

I read Acts 1 and 2 the other day, and something struck me for the first time. In these chapters, we see where 120 people were praying in the Upper Room, waiting for the promise of the Holy Spirit. Originally, when Jesus was resurrected, He appeared to the twelve and then to 500 of His followers (See 1 Cor. 15:5-6).

What strikes me is that Jesus appeared to 500 people, but only 120 actually made it to the Upper Room. Something happened along the way. The other 380 gave up or did not make it at all. What was the difference between the 120 and the others? What made these "Upper Room" Christians different from the rest?

One of the differences I see is that the 120 knew how to actively wait. The phrase "actively waiting" sounds like a contradiction of sorts. They were waiting for the Holy Spirit to show up, but it doesn't mean they weren't doing anything. In fact, they had turned their place of waiting into a place of prayer.

They also learned to persevere in prayer even when they did not see immediate results. I wonder, how many times in our lives have we given up on something when we were so close to a breakthrough? Lately, I've committed myself to persevere in more areas of my life. I do not want to stand before God one day and hear Him say, "I wanted to give you this, but you gave up too soon."

WHAT'S YOUR LABEL?

Then they reached Jericho, and as Jesus and his disciples left town, a large crowd followed him. A blind beggar named Bartimaeus (son of Timaeus) was sitting beside the road.
Mark 10:46

In Mark 10:46-52, we meet a guy named Bartimaeus. Timaeus means "unclean or contaminated." It could also mean "son of blindness." Imagine growing up with a last name that means "unclean or contaminated"? You know the kids at school picked on him!

He came from a contaminated background. Bartimaeus was literally blind, which means he couldn't see. Since he had no vision, he couldn't walk very well; thus, he had no future. His only hope was spending his life as a beggar.

Bartimaeus had one encounter with Jesus, and it changed his life. Bartimaeus wore a beggar's cloak, which identified him as a disabled person. It also protected him from the weather and helped him to collect alms. When Jesus called, Bartimaeus threw his beggar's cloak aside and ran to Him. When Jesus calls you to himself, you can throw away your old labels, and your life is changed. The truth sets you free. Be free today!

IGNORE THE HATERS AND NAYSAYERS!

But Jesus overheard them and said to Jairus, "Don't be afraid. Just have faith."
Mark 5:36

Anytime you attempt something for God, you're going to attract haters and naysayers. You can always tell a hater from ordinary people because they're too afraid to try something challenging. Haters will attack anyone who tries because they don't want to look bad. Successful people make haters uncomfortable.

Jesus ignored those who said it was too late and couldn't be done. He told Jairus to not be afraid and just believe. When we find ourselves in an impossible situation, we need to push through and ignore what other people say. Our situation was never dependent upon them anyway. If you have haters, it just means you're doing something right!

SURROUND YOURSELF WITH THE RIGHT PEOPLE

Then Jesus stopped the crowd and wouldn't let anyone go with him except Peter, James, and John (the brother of James).
Mark 5:37

As Jesus went to heal the daughter of Jairus, He did not take everyone with Him. He only took His inner circle. Jesus did not allow anyone to follow Him—only Peter, James, and John. He did not let the naysayers follow Him into the house. He didn't allow everyone to go with Him, only those He could trust.

We need to be more selective about who we talk to and who we allow to be with us in difficult situations. We only need to take those who can believe and have faith with us. It's not very smart to take your difficult situations to an unbeliever. Because they don't have the mind of Christ, we shouldn't be asking them for advice on our troubles.

SPEAK LIFE NOT DEATH

He went inside and asked, "Why all this commotion and weeping? The child isn't dead; she's only asleep."
Mark 5:39

When Jesus walked into this hopeless situation, He began to speak life and not death. Jesus began to speak faith over an impossible situation. He did not allow the circumstances of His current reality to dictate His faith. He chose faith over fear.

When you choose faith over fear, it doesn't mean you ignore the obvious; it means you choose to focus on how big your God is. There are moments when you have to tell your problems how big your God is. When facing an impossibility, it's easy to focus on the situation rather than the answer. Jesus is the answer to every test!

LET THEM LAUGH

The crowd laughed at him.
Mark 5:40

The last few days we've been talking about the story of Jesus raising Jairus' daughter from the dead. Yesterday, we spoke about speaking life and not death in difficult situations. When you do that, you need to be prepared for people to laugh at you. There are moments when people are going to mock your faith, and that's okay. It goes with the territory.

Don't expect everyone around you to agree with you or to be happy with you. The favor and anointing of God on your life will naturally attract jealousy and negativity from others. When Joseph told his brothers of his dream, they ridiculed him and eventually sold him into slavery. Don't be surprised if others around you are jealous of what God is doing in your life. It goes with the territory.

KICK OUT DOUBT AND UNBELIEF

But he made them all leave, and he took the girl's father and mother and his three disciples into the room where the girl was lying.
Mark 5:40

The miracle only came after Jesus put away doubt and unbelief. Even though the haters laughed at Jesus, He still saw the little girl raised from the dead. Jesus kicked out everyone in the house, except for His disciples and the girl's parents.

If you're going to see the miraculous in your life, you have to evict doubt and unbelief. This doesn't mean going home and kicking out your spouse. I know this is tempting for some of you! It means choosing not to focus on the impossibility but rather choosing to focus on the possibilities. All things are possible with God.

LEARN TO EXPECT THE UNEXPECTED

And the girl, who was twelve years old, immediately stood up and walked
around! They were overwhelmed and totally amazed.
Mark 5:42

This is the last devotional concerning Jesus raising Jairus' daughter from
the dead. We've talked about having haters, being laughed at, and
speaking life in impossible situations. In this final lesson, I want to
encourage you to expect the unexpected.

The Scripture says the girl "immediately stood up and walked
around." I suspect that was a sight to see! Everyone, except Jesus, was
surprised. He knew it was going to happen. He expected to see the miraculous. We need to start thinking and acting like this!

What would happen if we actually began to believe God for the
answer to our prayers? How might we pray differently if we knew the
impossible could be possible?

A CLOSED DOOR

A male and female of each kind entered, just as God had commanded Noah.
Then the LORD *closed the door behind them.*
Genesis 7:16

The story of Noah is an interesting one. Most people glance over the details and forget what really took place. It's an exciting story of faith and action in tandem.

I'll give you the Cliff Notes version. The earth was full of all kinds of evil, and the Lord was tired of it. So, God found a man who was righteous in his generation. He found Noah and told him to build an ark because of the coming rain. This sounded simple enough, but God told him to build an ark in the middle of a desert. To top it off, it had never rained before, and Noah had probably never seen a boat before.

Noah was in a tough spot. It seemed like the Lord had put him in a difficult situation. The funny thing is, Noah did nothing wrong to get there. He was only being obedient. If you're in a tough spot, maybe the Lord wants to do something new in your life.

Genesis 7:16 sums up the whole situation: "Then the Lord closed the door behind him." The Lord shut Noah into a hard place. How do we know this was a hard place?

It was a hard place because Noah and his family lived in a boat for over a year—with all kinds of animals. This was no Carnival Cruise Ship. There was no running water, electricity, elevators, internet, or modern amenities. The boat was loaded with animals! Noah had to take care of the animals, feed them, and nurture them. He had to put up with animals wanting to kill and eat each another. Noah had to learn how to operate a pooper scooper! This was no vacation cruise.

Noah was living in a difficult place, but he was going to a better place. When God puts you in a difficult position, He's preparing something better for you. Noah's trust in God went to a whole new level during this time. I'm sure there were days when he was ready to get off the boat, but he had to stay there until God released him. When God puts you in a difficult place, you need to stay there until He releases us. If you're facing difficulty in your life, you need to be obedient and wait for His directions. Many people interpret hardship in their lives as God's disapproval or punishment when actually He wants to do something new.

THAT'S GOOD RIGHT THERE!

Then God said, "Let the waters beneath the sky flow together into one place, so dry ground may appear." And that is what happened.
Genesis 1:9

According to Genesis, God created the earth in six days. If God is all-powerful and nothing is impossible for Him, why didn't He just make everything in one day? Indeed, if He had wanted to, He could have done so!

I think it's because He wanted to enjoy His work and enjoy the process. On days three, four, five, and six, He took a step back from His work and said, "That's good right there!" (Okay, maybe He didn't say it just like that, but He did say it was good!)

God took the time to reflect upon His work and to enjoy the process. When He created man, He said, "It was very good." Man was the pinnacle of God's work. He saved the best for last. I think God was modeling a life of work for us. I think He was trying to teach us to enjoy the ride and to enjoy the moments. I want to encourage you to take a few minutes today and enjoy just being in God's presence to reflect upon what He's done in your life. You might even need to say, "That's good right there!"

292

DANGEROUS TIMES

But when Rehoboam was firmly established and strong, he abandoned the Law of the LORD, and all Israel followed him in this sin.
2 Chronicles 12:1

The most dangerous time in a person's life is when things are going well and when the blessing of the Lord is readily apparent.

The blessings of God can complicate your life. When you are blessed, you tend not to need the Lord as much as you once did. It's a delicate position because you do not want to become too proud and too independent in thinking you have accomplished everything by your own hands. Humility and gratitude will keep your ego from swelling and from getting out of check. Never become strong enough that you no longer need God. If you do, it could lead to your downfall.

WHAT YOU THINK ABOUT JESUS MATTERS

She had heard about Jesus, so she came up behind him through the crowd and touched his robe. For she thought to herself, "If I can just touch his robe, I will be healed."
Mark 5:27-28

Miracles begin in the mind. Before the woman received her miracle, she first thought it was possible. Her only thought was that if she could get close enough to Jesus and touch His clothes, she would be healed.

What do you believe Jesus is capable of in your life? If He can do it for someone else, He can do it for you. If He has done it once, He can do it again.

294

IN-BETWEEN MIRACLES

Then the LORD said to Moses, "Why are you crying out to me? Tell the people to get moving!"
Exodus 14:15

This is an interesting verse because the Lord told them to quit crying over their situation and move on. They were crying over their hardships because they felt trapped between Egypt and the Red Sea. They were literally in-between miracles. They couldn't get to their Promised Land until they stopped crying about what they lost and the pain of the past. God doesn't mind if we grieve and mourn, but He won't let us live there. The writer of Psalms reminds us, "For his anger lasts only a moment, but his favor lasts a lifetime! Weeping may last through the night, but joy comes with the morning" (Psalm 30:5).

It's okay to grieve and lament the bad things that have happened to you. Maybe you're grieving through a divorce, dealing with a job loss, or a facing financial difficulty. No matter what happened to you in the past, you have to forgive yourself. You've been forgiven, and you don't have to keep feeling guilt and shame over your mistakes. God says, "Move on to the new things I have for you!"

HIS PRAISE SHOULD BE ON YOUR LIPS

I will praise the LORD at all times. I will constantly speak his praises. I will boast only in the LORD; let all who are helpless take heart. Come, let us tell of the LORD's greatness; let us exalt his name together.
Psalm 34:1-3

David says the praise of God should be on our lips. In other words, it shouldn't just be in our hearts, but it should be coming out of our mouths as well.

Why do we need to do this? Because we tend to believe and remember what we hear. Have you ever noticed how hard it is to remember a Scripture verse, but how easy it is to remember a famous movie line or a favorite worship song? Again, it's because we believe and remember what we hear.

The other reason His praise should be on our lips is for the benefit of hurting people around us. Your worship and your praise just might be what someone else needs to hear. It could be enough to lift their spirits and cause them to start rejoicing as well.

296

KEEP THE FIRE BURNING

"Every morning when Aaron maintains the lamps, he must burn fragrant incense on the altar. And each evening when he lights the lamps, he must again burn incense in the Lord's presence. This must be done from generation to generation."
Exodus 30:7-8

Scripture often compares prayer to incense that is a pleasing aroma to the Lord. In this Scripture, the Lord was teaching them how to keep the fire going in their lives. He instructed them to light incense in the morning and at twilight. In other words, they were to never stop praying (1 Thess. 5:17). The key was to continually seek God in prayer.

The fragrant incense was to be done in the morning because it was the first part of the day. God wants the first part of our day, not our leftovers. I don't think God will be mad at you if you choose to have a devotional time later in the day. I prefer the morning because it's the quietest part of my day, and if I wait too late, I usually won't do it because of the busyness of my schedule. I also do it because Scripture encourages us to "Seek the Kingdom of God above all else, and live righteously, and he will give you everything you need" (Matt. 6:33). When you make God's business your business, He will take care of your business.

CLOSE THE DOOR

Meanwhile, Elisha the prophet had summoned a member of the group of prophets. "Get ready to travel," he told him, "and take this flask of olive oil with you. Go to Ramoth-gilead, and find Jehu son of Jehoshaphat, son of Nimshi. Call him into a private room away from his friends, and pour the oil over his head. Say to him, 'This is what the LORD says: I anoint you to be the king over Israel.' Then open the door and run for your life!"
2 Kings 9:1-3

Jehu received his anointing to be king by going with the prophet to an inner room. He had to be separated from his companions before the oil could be poured over his head. In other words, we can't live and act like everyone else and expect to see the anointing operate in our lives. The inner room was a place of intimacy and privacy. He also went there because he needed to separate himself from the distractions and cares of this world. It was a secret place.

In the New Testament, when instructing His disciples about prayer, Jesus told His disciples to go into a room and shut the door behind them. Then, your Father who sees what you do in secret and will reward you for it. The reward is the anointing and presence of God in your life.

TEAR DOWN THE WALLS

Uzziah declared war on the Philistines and broke down the walls of Gath, Jabneh, and Ashdod. Then he built new towns in the Ashdod area and in other parts of Philistia.

2 Chronicles 26:6

In this passage, King Uzziah takes an offensive position against the enemy. He went out against the enemy in a deliberate manner. He went to tear down the walls that had been built up. These walls stood in the way of his kingdom's advancement. He didn't wait for the enemy to attack him. He took the fight to the enemy.

Rather than waiting around and playing defense, I wonder how often the Lord is waiting on us to take the fight to the enemy. Uzziah didn't wait for something to happen; he made it happen!

As believers, we need to quit playing it safe and believe God for bigger and better things. We need to believe God for the advancement of His Kingdom and begin to pray, "May your Kingdom come soon. May your will be done on earth, as it is in heaven" (Matthew 6:10).

SUCK IT UP BUTTERCUP!

Endure suffering along with me, as a good soldier of Christ Jesus. Soldiers don't get tied up in the affairs of civilian life, for then they cannot please the officer who enlisted them.
2 Timothy 2:3-4

Next to Jesus, no one else in Scripture understood suffering like the Apostle Paul. He certainly had a knack for it! In this passage, he's writing to his young protégé, Timothy. He wants us to understand that, as believers, we can expect hardship. He makes the comparison between a believer and a soldier. Soldiers go through boot camp to be trained so they can learn how to endure suffering. Ironically, those soldiers who want to be used in more significant ways, such as Navy Seals and other Special Forces operators, endure more training and hardship. During boot camp, soldiers are intentionally placed in difficult scenarios so they'll learn how to respond when they encounter adversity in the field of battle.

A good soldier also minds his own business and doesn't get caught up in civilian affairs. He does not focus on distractions, things out of his control, or something unrelated to his mission. When soldiers get distracted, people die.

As a believer, it's essential to understand that everyone will face hardships and difficulties. No one gets a free pass from pain. You can expect tribulation to come, but you can also know you can do all things through Christ, who gives you the strength you need. His grace is sufficient for you in every circumstance. If you're suffering today, please know the Lord is with you and will see you through it.

ESCAPE YOUR CAVE

One day the prophet Gad told David, "Leave the stronghold and return to the land of Judah." So David went to the forest of Hereth.

1 Samuel 22:5

God told David to leave the cave of Adullam and go into the land of Judah. David had been hiding in a cave of despair. It was known as the Cave of Adullam, and some scholars believe Adullam means "place of no foreseeable future." To say David was in a dark place in his life was an understatement. While running from Saul and escaping from Gath of the Philistines, he hit rock bottom. If he wasn't clinically depressed, he was close.

Ironically, the only word David received from the Lord was to leave the cave of Adullam and go into the land of Judah. Judah means "praise." Sometimes we have to praise our way out of the darkness. It's the opposite of what we would typically want to do. The easy thing to do would be to live in a cave of despair and complain about our situations. There are certainly times where we need to seek professional help for depression, but there are times when we just need to get in the presence of God and worship Jesus. Instead of complaining about our situations, we need to begin to praise the one who has the answer.

THE GREAT EXCHANGE

Don't worry about anything; instead, pray about everything. Tell God what you need, and thank him for all he has done. Then you will experience God's peace, which exceeds anything we can understand. His peace will guard your hearts and minds as you live in Christ Jesus.
Philippians 4:6-7

Over the years, as I have traveled on mission trips to other countries, I have always enjoyed a favorable exchange rate. The exchange is higher for us because the dollar is valued higher. Likewise, God's exchange rate is always better for us. We always come out for the better.

An exchange takes place in prayer. When we pray about everything and give thanks to God, He takes our burdens and petitions and exchanges them for His peace. Often we don't have peace because we are not praying and God does not have the opportunity to move in our circumstances. Jesus is the Prince of Peace, and when we seek Him in prayer, He takes our anxious thoughts and exchanges them for His peace.

The peace God gives transcends all understanding. In other words, when we are in the midst of a storm, we can rest and know Jesus is in control—we can walk on water if necessary! The storm might continue raging, but you can keep walking in the midst of it.

BE SHAMELESSLY AUDACIOUS!

But I tell you this—though he won't do it for friendship's sake, if you keep
knocking long enough, he will get up and give you whatever you need because
of your shameless persistence.
Luke 11:8

In this passage, Jesus is teaching His disciples about prayer. He tells the story of a friend who goes to a friend's house at midnight asking for bread to feed someone who has come to his house on a journey. It's hard to imagine the boldness it would take to go to a friend's house at midnight to borrow some bread or some eggs. Rather than suffer the embarrassment of not showing hospitality to his guest, the man decides to go to his friend's house and ask for what he needs.

The man's need did not compel the neighbor to meet his demand. The neighbor gave the man what he needed because of his boldness to ask at midnight. God certainly cares about our needs, but I think He wants us to have the shameless audacity to ask Him for things. Sometimes we are afraid to ask for big things because we fear that God won't answer. I would encourage you to keep knocking on heaven's door and to keep praying as long as it takes. Knock and the door will be opened to you.

303

YOU CAN HAVE IT ALL AND STILL HAVE NOTHING

So I decided there is nothing better than to enjoy food and drink and to find satisfaction in work. Then I realized that these pleasures are from the hand of God. For who can eat or enjoy anything apart from him?
Ecclesiastes 2:24-25

Presumably, the writer of Ecclesiastes was King Solomon. He was the wisest and wealthiest king who has ever lived. According to this passage, you can have it all and still have nothing. Stuff cannot satisfy you. Solomon says the best thing to do is to eat, drink, and enjoy life. This is coming from a man who spent most of his life building his own kingdom. No one had a greater empire than he did. He spent seven years building the temple and fourteen years building his palace. This does not include his other building projects as well. If he were here today, he would encourage you not to get so caught up in building that you don't enjoy the present. Sometimes the best thing you can do is to be in the moment. Be present now.

HOSPITALITY OPENS DOORS

The LORD appeared again to Abraham near the oak grove belonging to Mamre. One day Abraham was sitting at the entrance to his tent during the hottest part of the day. He looked up and noticed three men standing nearby. When he saw them, he ran to meet them and welcomed them, bowing low to the ground.

Genesis 18:1-2

In the Middle East, especially in desert places, people would typically reserve their outdoor work for early in the mornings or in the evenings. During the hottest part of the day, they would try to do as little as possible. The heat in the desert is more than just uncomfortable; it can be deadly.

The Lord appeared to Abraham during the hottest part of the day. Abraham was over seventy-five years old, so he was no spring chicken! When God showed up to meet with Abraham, it was an inconvenience and an interruption to his day. Abraham could have made an excuse about the heat, but instead, he hurried from his tent to meet them, and bowed down to show them respect.

Abraham took the time to feed them, wash their feet, and give them water to drink. In other words, he showed them hospitality. Ironically, after he showed them hospitality, the Lord gave him the revelation that they would have a son within the following year. God had answered their prayers!

Showing hospitality opens the way for God to reveal himself and answer our prayers. Abraham didn't hold back when he showed them hospitality. He gave them his very best. He offered a "choice tender calf" not his leftovers. When we offer hospitality to others in need, God has a way of answering our prayers.

305

RENEWED LIKE AN EAGLE

He fills my life with good things. My youth is renewed like the eagle's!
Psalm 103:5

God expertly designed the eagle's feathers to protect them from the weather and the water, but eventually they wear out. Over time, eagles lose their worn out feathers, a process known as molting. Young eagles go through four different plumages before becoming mature adult eagles. After reaching the adult stage, most eagles will molt once a year. They lose their old feathers but, in the process, gain new ones that enable them to fly and glide better. The molting process is a renewal process.

As followers of Christ, we might go through a renewal process. Often we need to shed old things that hinder us, such as insecurities, failures, shame, and past sins. God removes these things from our lives to help us soar. Paul later wrote, "This means that anyone who belongs to Christ has become a new person. The old life is gone; a new life has begun" (2 Cor. 5:17)! In the end, God satisfies our desires with good things so He can take us to new heights and help us soar above the storms of life.

306

FAVOR IS COMPLICATED

But the LORD was with Joseph in the prison and showed him his faithful love.
And the LORD made Joseph a favorite with the prison warden. Before long, the
warden put Joseph in charge of all the other prisoners and over everything that
happened in the prison.
Genesis 39:21-22

The favor of God was on Joseph's life. The more favor Joseph received, the more responsibility he was given. In Potiphar's house, he enjoyed God's favor and was given the responsibility of managing the entire household. While in prison, he enjoyed the favor of God as well, but was given the responsibility of managing all the affairs of the prison. Favor is not fair, and it's not always fun. The favor of God will complicate your life. Be careful what you ask for!

REDEFINING DISCIPLINE

"I correct and discipline everyone I love. So be diligent and turn from your indifference."
Revelation 3:19

Discipline is an expression of love. To be disciplined by someone, you must be in a relationship with them; you must be in proximity with them. You only discipline people with whom you have a relationship.

I don't discipline other people's children. I make it a habit to only discipline my own children. I can discipline my own children because I have a relationship with them. They know I love them, and I have expressed my love for them on multiple occasions. If I were to discipline my children, but they didn't know that I love them, they would interpret my discipline as doing something to them rather than for them. That is how the Lord views discipline. When He disciplines us, He does it for our good. Discipline is good for us because it helps us mature and keeps us off the pathway of sin.

LIVING BETWEEN THE PROMISE AND THE MIRACLE

That same day Pharaoh sent this order to the Egyptian slave drivers and the Israelite foremen: "Do not supply any more straw for making bricks. Make the people get it themselves! But still require them to make the same number of bricks as before. Don't reduce the quota. They are lazy. That's why they are crying out, 'Let us go and offer sacrifices to our God.' Load them down with more work. Make them sweat! That will teach them to listen to lies!"
Exodus 5:6-9

In Exodus 4, the Israelites received the promise of deliverance, but things got worse before they got better. Pharaoh began to put more pressure on them to meet their quota. At one point, they had to make bricks and gather the straw. By the end of Exodus 5, the Israelites were mad at Moses and blamed him for their troubles. Moses went back to his prayer closet and strengthened himself in the Lord. He had to know the Lord was going to keep His promise because, at this point, the people were too tired and discouraged to believe otherwise.

The key to standing during the in-between time is standing with the Lord. Sometimes, like Moses, it's just you standing with the Lord. The good news is that anytime we stand with the Lord, we are in the majority.

Scripture teaches that God does what pleases Him. He doesn't wait for the votes to come in, and He doesn't have to have a second opinion. His is the only opinion that matters. The Bible teaches that once we've done all we know to do, then we just keep standing.

309

TAKE NOTE OF THIS

Understand this, my dear brothers and sisters: You must all be quick to listen, slow to speak, and slow to get angry.

James 1:19

We need to be the first to listen and the last to speak. We should be quick to listen and take our time when speaking. Anger is not a fruit of the righteous life. Listening means we are seeking to understand, not preparing to speak. We need to make it a point to listen more and react less.

How would listening more and talking less change your relationships?

310

WAIT FOR IT!

Then Moses climbed up the mountain, and the cloud covered it. And the glory of the LORD settled down on Mount Sinai, and the cloud covered it for six days. On the seventh day the LORD called to Moses from inside the cloud.

Exodus 24:15-16

In this chapter, the Lord instructed Moses to come up to the mountain so that He could give him the Ten Commandments. Moses went up the mountain, and he waited seven days before the Lord finally spoke to him. The text never says why Moses had to wait seven days, but I suspect the Lord was testing him. I think the Lord wanted to see how long Moses would be willing to wait. You'll only sacrifice your time for what's important to you.

Moses was so desperate to hear from the Lord that he was willing to stay as long as it took. Let's be honest; most of us would have probably given up after the first couple of hours. We might have stayed for one day, but would we wait for seven days?

As believers, we must come to the place where we are hungry and desperate enough for God that we are willing to wait as long as it takes.

311

WASH YOUR HANDS!

*Next Moses placed the washbasin between the Tabernacle and the altar. He
filled it with water so the priests could wash themselves. Moses and Aaron and
Aaron's sons used water from it to wash their hands and feet. Whenever they
approached the altar and entered the Tabernacle, they washed themselves, just
as the LORD had commanded Moses.*
Exodus 40:30-32

In coming through the most recent pandemic, there is one thing we've all
learned to do: wash our hands! We quickly discovered that washing our
hands should be a normal process in daily life.

Every time the priests went to minister before the Lord, they washed
their hands and feet. They would not dare approach the altar of God with
dirt on their hands. Their washing was not a one-time event; it was a
daily process. Likewise, repentance is a daily process, not a one-time
event at the altar. At salvation, we are justified and made righteous before
God because Jesus paid the price for our sins with His blood. Even
though we are justified, we still deal with sin, and this necessitates the
daily washing of our spirits.

312

IT'S A FIXED FIGHT!

But the Lord *said to Joshua, "I have given you Jericho, its king, and all its*
strong warriors."
Joshua 6:2

The Lord was teaching Joshua that the battle had already been won. In
the eyes of the Lord, it was a done deal. Joshua had to believe it before he
could see it. In the kingdom, believing is seeing.

As believers, we also operate from that same vantage point. We
operate from a position of victory because Jesus has already won it all for
us. Sure, there are still battles to fight, but the war has already been won.
We are just waiting for the walls to start coming down. We are fighting a
fixed fight. Jesus already won the battle on the cross of victory.

313

HE HAS WHAT YOU NEED

By his divine power, God has given us everything we need for living a godly life. We have received all of this by coming to know him, the one who called us to himself by means of his marvelous glory and excellence.

2 Peter 1:3

Everything we need in life is found in our relationship with Jesus. He is the answer to every test, and He has what we need. If we seek Him, we will have what we need.

By God's power, we have everything we need to live a godly life. It comes through our relationship and knowledge of Him. We can't get what we need for life apart from our relationship with Jesus. Power gained in any other way is a counterfeit. He called us because of His glory and goodness toward us.

314

GATHER WHAT YOU NEED

So the people of Israel did as they were told. Some gathered a lot, some only a little. But when they measured it out, everyone had just enough. Those who gathered a lot had nothing left over, and those who gathered only a little had enough. Each family had just what it needed. Then Moses told them, "Do not keep any of it until morning."
Exodus 16:17-19

While the people of Israel wandered in the desert, God supernaturally provided manna, a type of bread, for the people. Every morning, the Israelites had to go out and gather their manna. God supernaturally provided the bread every day, but they still had to go out and gather what they needed. The bread was only good for one day. If they tried to keep some for the next day, it would rot.

We can learn a few things from this passage as it relates to our lives. While we do not need to gather physical bread every day, we must gather our own spiritual food—often called the bread of life. Jesus referred to himself as "the bread of life" (John 6:35). As we read our Bible and spend time with Jesus, He gives us the spiritual nourishment we need. No one would eat one meal a week and consider that enough nutrition for the week, yet many believers will go to church on Sunday and attempt to live on that for the rest of the week. It's no wonder a lot of believers are walking around anemic and spiritually malnourished!

The Scripture also says, "And as the sun became hot, the flakes they had not picked up melted and disappeared" (Exodus 16:21). Fresh manna must be harvested every day because when things get hot, it melts away. The busier we become, the more we must go to God and get what we need for the day. We are too busy not to pray. Jesus only asks that we come to get what we need for that day. We don't have to stock up or hoard what we have because He has enough for tomorrow, the next day, and the day after. All we must do is come to Him for what we need today.

DON'T GET DISTRACTED

Saul and David were now on opposite sides of a mountain. Just as Saul and his men began to close in on David and his men, an urgent message reached Saul that the Philistines were raiding Israel again.
1 Samuel 23:26-27

In this passage, Saul was so distracted with capturing and killing David that it left Israel unguarded and open to the enemy's attack. When kings get distracted, it opens the door for an enemy attack.

As leaders and as parents, it's easy to get distracted by the wrong things in life. You might be chasing money, bad relationships, or a plethora of other things. In this case, Saul's jealousy and envy of David caused him to become distracted. Rather than leading Israel into battle against their enemies, he was leading them on a wild goose chase. Saul was going in circles chasing one man, David. If you aren't careful, you can get so distracted by the wrong things that you find yourself going in circles or realize that you keep circling the same mountain. The only way to get out of going in circles is to get off the hamster wheel and refocus on your calling and on what is truly important. If you've been going in circles, you need to ask the Lord to help you get focused on Him and His purposes for your life.

BROKEN BUT NOT FORGOTTEN

*The king then asked him, "Is anyone still alive from Saul's family? If so, I want
to show God's kindness to them." Ziba replied, "Yes, one of Jonathan's sons is still
alive. He is crippled in both feet." "Where is he?" the king asked. "In Lo-debar,"
Ziba told him, "at the home of Makir son of Ammiel." So David sent for him and
brought him from Makir's home. His name was Mephibosheth; he was
Jonathan's son and Saul's grandson. When he came to David, he bowed low to
the ground in deep respect. David said, "Greetings, Mephibosheth."
Mephibosheth replied, "I am your servant."*
2 Samuel 9:3-6

When David became king, he remembered a vow he had made to
Jonathan. He vowed to always show kindness to Jonathan's family. This
would have been an unusual vow because, in those days, when a new
king came into power, he would wipe out the previous royal family, especially all the males. This was done to prevent the last king's family from
staging a coup.

Mephibosheth was a son of Jonathan and a grandson of King Saul.
When he was young, his nurse was carrying him. In her haste, she
dropped him and he became crippled in both feet. He lived in Lo Debar,
which means "not having" or "no pasture." In other words, he grew up

broken and in poverty. It's hardly the life you would dream of for the grandson of a king.

David had Mephiboshet brought to the city of Jerusalem, which means "city of peace." In one day, King David restored everything that was lost to Mephibosheth! David fulfilled his vow to Jonathan. He restored the family land to Mephibosheth and allowed him to eat at the king's table—just like all the other king's sons.

We can take away a few things from this text. Despite being broken and lame, Mephibosheth could still eat at the king's table. Although Mephibosheth came from a place of "not having" and "no pasture," it didn't mean he had come to the end of his story. God had a place of peace and provision for him. In the end, Mephibosheth wasn't perfect and didn't have it all together, but he still sat with the other king's sons. His honor and self-image were restored. Mephibosheth had a rough start at life, but it did not end that way. When God is writing your story, there's always the chance of "happily ever after!"

KING FOR A DAY OR KING FOR A LIFETIME?

*About that time David's son Adonijah, whose mother was Haggith, began
boasting, "I will make myself king." So he provided himself with chariots and
charioteers and recruited fifty men to run in front of him. Now his father, King
David, had never disciplined him at any time, even by asking, "Why are you
doing that?" Adonijah had been born next after Absalom, and he was very
handsome.*

1 Kings 1:5-6

David's son, Adonijah, was the second born after Absalom. According to
tradition, he would have been next in line to be king after David. He
would have been man's pick. He was good-looking, had money, was
charismatic, aggressive, and a good leader. He was the total package,
except he wasn't God's pick.

Solomon was God's pick because his heart was different. Scripture
says Nathan, the prophet, and Abiathar, the priest, anointed him with oil
and put him on the king's mule.

One guy had all the goods; the other guy had the anointing. Adonijah
rode in a chariot, which was more about power and putting on a show. In
contrast, Solomon rode the king's mule, which symbolized humility,

honor, and royalty. When you're anointed, you don't have to tell everyone. The anointing speaks for itself.

You may not be man's pick or have all the talents and gifts, but if you're anointed, God can use you. The anointing is what makes the difference in our lives. There must be an anointing on our lives if we are going to do what we are called to do. Adonijah was a pseudo king for a few hours, but Solomon would be king for 40 years. Solomon made his own mistakes and chased many wrong things, but he still had the anointing on his life. When you're man's pick, you can be king for a day, but when you're God's pick, you can be king for a lifetime.

318

BE THE EXAMPLE

Amaziah did what was pleasing in the LORD's sight, but not like his ancestor David. Instead, he followed the example of his father, Joash.

2 Kings 14:3

Children follow your example, not your advice. Throughout the books of 1 and 2 Kings, the children followed the example of their fathers, whether good or bad. For children, parents serve as the primary example of how to follow God.

The question remains, "What kind of example are you being to your children?" Really think about this! Scripture says that in "everything," the children followed their father's example. As parents, like it or not, we are the primary example of God to our children. You only get one shot at it, so make it count!

IN THE COURSE OF TIME

After this, David defeated and subdued the Philistines by conquering
Gath and its surrounding towns.
1 Chronicles 18:1

This chapter details David's victories while he was king of Israel. He defeated Goliath in one battle, but the rest of his enemies took time. He methodically kept getting up every day and taking new territory from the enemy. He never gave up, even when he didn't see big results.

David wasn't an overnight success. He reigned 40 years as king of Israel and he took the long view of life. He willingly invested himself in God's Kingdom and chose to spend his life for the next generation. Anything worth accomplishing in God's Kingdom is going to take more than your lifetime. What will your legacy be?

320

HE'S STILL WORKING

Your road led through the sea, your pathway through the mighty
waters—a pathway no one knew was there! You led your people along
that road like a flock of sheep, with Moses and Aaron as their shepherds.
Psalm 77:19-20

Over the years, I've heard many well-meaning people say, "God will never give you more than you can handle!" This sounds good in theory, but it's not true. If you're a student of the Bible, you'll quickly realize that most people who were used of God were always in over their heads. That's why God does miracles. That's why God gains glory for himself. When we are in over our heads, we confess our need for Him. When we are weak, He is strong.

When we walk through the mighty waters, we must depend completely on God. It often makes us scared and leaves us feeling overwhelmed. The good news, according to this Scripture, is that He is leading us through these difficult places. He never leaves us and He never abandons us. Even though the Israelites could not see His footsteps, they could see the evidence of God's work in their lives. Sometimes we may not see Him, but we can see the evidence of God in our lives. Your survival is evidence of God's hand on your life.

THE FOUNDATION OF PRAYER

So you have not received a spirit that makes you fearful slaves. Instead, you received God's Spirit when he adopted you as his own children. Now we call him, "Abba, Father."
Romans 8:15

Our foundation of prayer starts with a relationship with the Father. Many people, I'm convinced, do not pray because they do not know the heart of the Father toward them. Many believers view God as a mean tyrant, which results in a fearful relationship. Truth be told, many of us did not have good relationships with our fathers, and we often project this onto our relationship with our Heavenly Father.

When you are born again, God adopts you into His family. You become one of His children and an heir of Jesus Christ. As adopted children, we have all the same rights and privileges as a natural child. As His children, the good news is that we can call Him Father, and He is there for us and will take care of us. As a child of God, you no longer have to fear him because you're no longer an enemy; you are a son or daughter (Romans 5:10; Colossians 1:21)!

THE SPIRIT ENABLES YOU

And everyone present was filled with the Holy Spirit and began speaking in other languages, as the Holy Spirit gave them this ability.

Acts 2:4

The Holy Spirit is the divine enabler in our lives. Enable means to give someone the authority or means to do something. The Spirit enables us to do what we cannot do on our own. He not only provides us with the power to do it, but He gives us the means to do it.

In the book of Acts, the Holy Spirit also enabled them to speak in other tongues. He still does the same today. If you're not filled with the Holy Spirit, take a moment and invite the Holy Spirit to fill you with His presence and to enable you to receive the gift of speaking in other tongues. The Holy Spirit wants to fill you with His power and grace to do what He's called you to do. All you have to do is ask!

Also, if you're facing a challenging situation in your life, take a moment this morning to ask the Holy Spirit for the divine enablement to do what you cannot do on your own. The Holy Spirit still does miracles, and He wants to do them through you!

A HAND UP, NOT A HANDOUT!

I am not afraid of ten thousand enemies who surround me on every side. Arise,
O LORD! Rescue me, my God! Slap all my enemies in the face! Shatter the teeth
of the wicked!
Psalm 3:6-7

Peter and John were on their way to prayer and had likely passed this man on many occasions, but today was different. It was different because now they had been filled with the Holy Spirit, and their eyes had been opened to the lost and hurting people around them.

The broken man was not given a handout but a hand up. He was taken by the right hand and pulled up. As leaders and as believers, who are we pulling up around us? Are we only paying attention to our own world and our own circumstances, or are we reaching out to pull up those around us? Who are you taking the time to notice?

324

OTHER PEOPLE NOTICE

The members of the council were amazed when they saw the boldness of Peter and John, for they could see that they were ordinary men with no special training in the Scriptures. They also recognized them as men who had been with Jesus.
Acts 4:13

Other people notice when you spend time with Jesus. When you spend time with Jesus, you begin to act like Him and talk like Him. You begin to have more courage and walk in a new level of boldness in your life. You even start to take on His personality and mannerisms. You become a new creation.

Can your family and coworkers tell when you've been with Jesus? I know one thing. My family can tell when I haven't been with Jesus! One day several years ago, I was having a rough day, and my wife asked, "You've been cranky lately, have you been spending enough time with Jesus?" Unfortunately, she was right! Can the people around you tell the difference when you've been with Jesus?

COLLAPSED FOUNDATIONS

The foundations of law and order have collapsed. What can the righteous do? But the LORD is in his holy Temple; the LORD still rules from heaven. He watches everyone closely, examining every person on earth.
Psalm 11:3-4

We live in perilous times. The days are not getting easier; they're getting more evil. Jesus warned us of this when He said there would be an increase in wickedness in the last days (Matthew 24:12). It feels like the foundation of our society is crumbling beneath us. The righteous are no longer celebrated, but rather mocked and ridiculed by those who promote evil. Where do we turn? What comfort can we have during this time?

This psalm reminds us that when we are shaken, God is not. He's still on the throne, and He's still sovereign over all the earth. He's still seated on His throne. He's not worried; He's not up pacing the floor. He's sitting because He's in control. God always gets the last word! In the end, He will judge those who do evil, and He will get the final say in every situation.

326

YOU CANNOT BE STOPPED!

"So my advice is, leave these men alone. Let them go. If they are planning and
doing these things merely on their own, it will soon be overthrown. But if it is
from God, you will not be able to overthrow them. You may even find yourselves
fighting against God!"
Acts 5:38-39

The apostles had been arrested for sharing their faith and were now on trial for being witnesses of Jesus. They were able to do this because their purpose had originated from God. They were not pursuing a human endeavor but a divine endeavor.

Our purposes in life must originate from God and be found in Him. All things must work out for our good when we are called according to His purpose (Romans 8:28). If it hasn't worked out for our good, it means God is still working things out. If your purpose is from God, then you cannot fail. You cannot be stopped! When God is for you, no one can be against you (Romans 8:31).

BE CAREFUL WHO SURROUNDS YOU

But Peter asked them all to leave the room; then he knelt and prayed. Turning to the body he said, "Get up, Tabitha." And she opened her eyes! When she saw Peter, she sat up!

Acts 9:40

Before Peter prayed for the dead woman, he sent out all the widows and all those who had been weeping over her. Interestingly, he separated himself from those who were mourning and had experienced death. Apparently, it matters how much faith is in the room.

Carefully select the people you allow to surround your life. Sometimes you have to separate yourself from the crowd if you want to see the miraculous. Peter's response to a crisis wasn't weeping but a posture of prayer.

328

BE A WITNESS, NOT A PROSECUTOR

But the voice spoke again: "Do not call something unclean if God has made it clean."
Acts 10:15

God decides who is clean or unclean, not us. As believers, God has called us to be witnesses, not prosecutors.

Scripture reminds us that man looks at outward appearances while God looks at the heart. We can easily get too focused on people's appearances, especially when they do not look, dress, or talk like us. They might even be of a different political persuasion. Don't get hung up on appearances or personalities. Ask the Lord to help you love your neighbors as yourself. Either way, God still loves them and died for them.

LIVE UNTIL YOU DIE!

This is not a reference to David, for after David had done the will of God in his own generation, he died and was buried with his ancestors, and his body decayed.
Acts 13:36

God had a purpose for David for his generation. His purpose was to serve as a king and leader for Israel. Most of us will never be a king, but we do have a purpose. Your purpose is tailor-fitted for your life and your gifts. God has a particular purpose for each one of us for our generation. Our job is to discover our purpose and to serve our generation. David died after he fulfilled his purpose. Likewise, you won't die one day sooner than when your purpose is fulfilled. In the meantime, live until you die!

330

FAITH MUST BE DEMONSTRATED

While they were at Lystra, Paul and Barnabas came upon a man with crippled feet. He had been that way from birth, so he had never walked. He was sitting and listening as Paul preached. Looking straight at him, Paul realized he had faith to be healed. So Paul called to him in a loud voice, "Stand up!" And the man jumped to his feet and started walking.
Acts 14:8-10

Paul saw the man's faith. Faith isn't just a thought; it's something that must be demonstrated. Faith is dead without good works (James 2:26).

There are times when we need to align our faith with what we say we believe. I had a professor who would say, "We must put our boots on and walk out our faith!" In other words, get up and do something!

We need to step out in faith and take a risk for God. Sometimes, while waiting for God to show us the way, He's waiting for us to take the first step. How can you demonstrate your faith in God today? What has He been asking you to do?

331

DON'T GET TOO COMFORTABLE

Afterward Paul felt compelled by the Spirit to go over to Macedonia and Achaia before going to Jerusalem. "And after that," he said, "I must go on to Rome!"
Acts 19:21

Paul enjoyed great ministry success in Ephesus. People were getting healed by touching Paul's handkerchiefs, and scores of people were coming to the Lord. Even though he had incredible results there and saw many extraordinary miracles, he did not allow himself to get too comfortable there. He pushed for new territory in his life and ministry. He wanted to take the gospel to Rome, and Paul wouldn't allow his present successes to hinder him.

As a believer, I want to continually grow and push forward into new territory in my life. As leaders, God has called us to comfort the afflicted and to afflict the comfortable! It's too easy to get complacent with things in our lives.

332

WHO ARE YOU FOLLOWING?

Ahaziah was twenty-two years old when he became king, and he reigned in Jerusalem one year. His mother was Athaliah, a granddaughter of King Omri. Ahaziah also followed the evil example of King Ahab's family, for his mother encouraged him in doing wrong. He did what was evil in the LORD's sight, just as Ahab's family had done. They even became his advisers after the death of his father, and they led him to ruin.

2 Chronicles 22:2-4

Ahaziah was twenty-two years old when he became king. It's hard to imagine being that young and being a king over a nation. At twenty-two years of age, I had no business trying to lead a ministry, much less trying to be a king. As a young and inexperienced leader, he should have surrounded himself with seasoned and godly leaders.

Ahaziah's reign only lasted one year. His life did not have to end the way it did, but unfortunately, he followed the wrong crowd to his own undoing. We must understand that who we follow will influence our final outcome.

333

DO NOT MINGLE!

Israel failed to destroy the nations in the land, as the Lord *had commanded them. Instead, they mingled among the pagans and adopted their evil customs.*
Psalm 106:34-35

The word "mingle" means to mix together. It implies becoming intertwined and mixed up with something. It's hard to mingle without picking up properties and traits of the other elements.

In this passage, the Lord was rebuking Israel because they chose to mingle with the sinful nations rather than destroy them. You can't mingle with sin and expect to remain untainted by it. If you're playing around with secret sin in your life, you need to cut it out and put it to death. You cannot continue to fool around with sin. Sin is subtle because you can fool yourself into thinking you can handle it and stop at any time. Unfortunately, sin has an insatiable appetite and will not stop until it destroys your life. The only way to deal with sin is to crucify it.

FOR SUCH A TIME AS THIS

"If you keep quiet at a time like this, deliverance and relief for the Jews will arise from some other place, but you and your relatives will die. Who knows if perhaps you were made queen for just such a time as this?"
Esther 4:14

You are not where you are by accident. You were born in this generation and in this time period because God has a plan and a purpose for your life. It's easy to buy into the lie that you're too old or that you have missed an opportunity in life. There is more ahead of you than what is behind you.

Someone around you is depending on you to lift your voice and not be silent. At the significant risk of her own life, Esther went to the king and lifted up her voice regarding the destruction of the Jews. She was not there by accident. God strategically positioned Esther as the queen at that particular time in history.

God has also placed you where you are so you can serve others. Don't think for a moment that just because you're not in full-time vocational ministry that your calling is not important. God has strategically positioned you to be the best teacher, medical professional, accountant, police officer, or other professional in your given context. The people around you need you. You could be the voice of deliverance for those with whom you work. Pray and ask the Lord today to use you to bring deliverance to someone in your sphere of influence. You have been brought to a royal position for such a time as this!

FRIENDS IN HIGH PLACES

Even now my witness is in heaven. My advocate is there on high. My friends scorn me, but I pour out my tears to God. I need someone to mediate between God and me, as a person mediates between friends.
Job 16:19-21

You have a friend in high places, and His name is Jesus. He is your advocate who stands before God making intercession for you (Romans 8:34). Because He is your friend, He can stand before the Lord pleading your case.

You've heard it said, "It's about who you know." Indeed, this is true when it comes to God. Our advocate is a friend that sticks closer than a brother. Furthermore, our Advocate is related to the Judge! You can walk around with your head held high, knowing you are favored and loved by God. You do not have to earn His love because Christ has already paid the price for your sins. Your steps should be a little lighter today as you walk in this truth.

THE LORD WILL VINDICATE YOU

Then he sent someone to Egypt ahead of them—Joseph, who was sold as a slave. They bruised his feet with fetters and placed his neck in an iron collar. Until the time came to fulfill his dreams, the LORD *tested Joseph's character.*
Psalm 105:17-19

When Potiphar's wife tried to tempt Joseph, he resisted her and ran out of the house. In the end, he was thrown into prison for doing the right thing.

There will be moments in your life when you do the right thing, and it costs you dearly. Joseph's integrity cost him a job. Rather than lash out, he left his case in the hands of God. While in prison, he kept serving the Lord. His ability to interpret dreams and to hear from God brought about his promotion. In the end, the word of the Lord vindicated him.

If you're in an unfair situation today, you can rest assured that God sees your situation and He will vindicate you. Your job is to keep serving the people around you while not allowing the harmful actions of others to develop a root of bitterness in your heart. If you don't become bitter, God can make things better!

YOU HAVE A TEACHER

My suffering was good for me, for it taught me to pay attention to your decrees.
Psalm 119:71

Pain has a way of getting our attention. In the human body, pain acts like a warning light on the car's dashboard. In essence, pain is a gift because it lets us know that something needs attention.

Likewise, pain is a good teacher. It often shares lessons that we do not easily forget. Pain's lessons have a long shelf life, and the lessons rarely expire. When we experience pain, it teaches us that we do not want to go through a particular situation again. In the parable of the Prodigal Son, the father allows the child to experience pain so the son will come back to his senses. Pain has a way of drawing us back toward a loving God and His Word. If you're experiencing pain today, I would encourage you to run toward the Father and allow Him to embrace you and to cover you with His robe of righteousness.

SHARE YOUR STORIES

Let each generation tell its children of your mighty acts; let them proclaim your power.
Psalm 145:4

As I work with emerging leaders, it's easy to look at their age and compare myself to them. Unfortunately, we live in a society that worships youthfulness and tolerates age. While I may not be able to do the things that I used to do, I am reminded that they need what I have in my life. The younger generation needs to hear my stories.

Don't be afraid to share your stories. The next generation needs to hear your testimony. Your story will give someone the courage to attempt something great for God. It just might be the encouragement they need to hear so they don't give up on a situation but decide to press on until they see the breakthrough.

Every Joshua needs a Moses; every Elisha needs an Elijah; and every Timothy needs a Paul. Be that person for someone today!

WORSHIP IS YOUR WEAPON!

Let the praises of God be in their mouths, and a sharp sword in their hands—to execute vengeance on the nations and punishment on the peoples, to bind their kings with shackles and their leaders with iron chains, to execute the judgment written against them. This is the glorious privilege of his faithful ones.
Psalm 149:6-9

Worship is warfare. Your worship is your weapon. Your praise is a weapon that binds the enemy. Your worship ties the hands of the enemy in your life. When you open your mouth to praise the Lord, you are doing battle against an unseen enemy. That is why the enemy will go to any lengths to distract you during worship. This is not a coincidence. It's the enemy's tactic to silence God's people.

When Saul was being tormented by evil spirits, it was David's worship that brought him relief. When you're being tormented by the enemy, your worship will cause the enemy to flee and the heaviness to lift. If you're feeling heaviness or despair today, take a few minutes and lift your hands in worship to the Lord. When you lift up your hands, the Lord will reach down with His!

340

GIVE FREELY

Give freely and become more wealthy; be stingy and lose everything.
Proverbs 11:24

At first glance, this proverb seems counterintuitive. How can a person give freely and yet gain more? In God's Kingdom, generosity is always rewarded. The world tells us to hoard and to selfishly hold on to what we have. We are taught to have a scarcity mentality. When we have a scarcity mentality, we believe there's not more where that came from. When we have a Kingdom mentality, we trust that God has a limitless supply and there's always more where that came from.

I want to encourage you to be generous and to test God in this area of your life. Giving is the only area in our life where we are told to test God (Malachi 3:10). I promise you that you cannot out give God. He can do more than you can ask, think, or imagine. Give God a try with your finances. You won't be disappointed.

341

QUIT TALKING AND START WORKING

Work brings profit, but mere talk leads to poverty!
Proverbs 14:23

The famous General Patton knew a thing or two about getting things done. He once said, "A good plan violently executed now is better than a perfect plan executed next week." He understood that good intention is never enough to get something done. At some point, you're going to have to put on your work boots and get to work.

God does not bless laziness. Many people are sitting around waiting for God to bless them with opportunities. Opportunity comes to the prepared. Scripture clearly teaches that God blesses the work of our hands (Deut. 28:12; Psalm 90:17). God cannot bless what you're not doing.

BORROWED FAITH

Gehazi hurried on ahead and laid the staff on the child's face, but nothing happened. There was no sign of life. He returned to meet Elisha and told him, "The child is still dead."

2 Kings 4:31

Gehazi couldn't raise the boy from the dead. He could borrow Elisha's staff, but he couldn't borrow his faith. You cannot live on someone else's faith. Faith must become personal in your life. It must be cultivated in your own walk with God. Gehazi was around the presence of God and witnessed Elisha perform many miracles, but he never did one of his own. At some point, we cannot live on our parent's faith or our pastor's faith. We must develop our own relationship with God.

343

YOU ARE NOT WHO YOU ARE TODAY

*The angel of the Lord appeared to him and said, "Mighty hero, the
Lord is with you!"*
Judges 6:12

The Lord saw Gideon for who he could be, not for who he was at the
moment. It's incredible to think that the Lord sees what is possible in our
lives rather than how He found us. I remember when the Lord found me.
I was one messed-up teenager. He saw me for who I was going to be, and
He does the same for you.

344

BECAUSE YOU SAY SO

"Master," Simon replied, "we worked hard all last night and didn't catch a thing.
But if you say so, I'll let the nets down again."
Luke 5:5

The disciples had been working all night and caught nothing. They were professional fishermen and had the best equipment, and yet they caught nothing.

Maybe you feel like the disciples. You've been working hard, but for some reason, you feel like you've been spinning your wheels and not getting anywhere. Their situation changed when Jesus got in their boat. He gave them one strategy that would change how their day started. I want to encourage you to lean into the Holy Spirit this morning and ask Him for divine counsel and wisdom for your day. Ask Him to give you the strategies you need to be successful and prosperous on your day. One word from the Lord can change your circumstances!

345

BUT THE CHURCH...

But while Peter was in prison, the church prayed very earnestly for him.
Acts 12:5

In this verse, the phrase "the church prayed" caught my attention. The Apostle Peter found himself in trouble for witnessing. He had been in trouble for a couple of days, and the night before he was to go to trial, an angel of the Lord showed up and delivered him from prison.

In the natural, Peter was in a hopeless situation. However, in the supernatural, anything was possible. While the church could have been sleeping, they were up praying. There are times in your life when you must force yourself to roll out of bed and get up and pray. Someone's life could be depending on it. My pastor always says, "You can either rollover or you can roll out." As long as the church was praying, Peter had a chance. As long as you have a prayer, you have a chance!

DON'T BE A WANDERER

So Cain left the Lord's presence and settled in the land of Nod, east of Eden.
Genesis 4:16

As a result of Cain's sin of killing his brother, he was banished from the Lord's presence. He lived in the land of Nod, which means "to wander." To live in the land of Nod is to live a wandering life. Sin in our lives causes us to live outside the presence of God. It acts as a divider between the Lord and us. Too many people choose to live in Nod because of their sin, and they end up wandering through life without the Lord's direction and purpose. God never intended for Cain to live in Nod. The Good News is that Jesus paid the price for our sins, and we no longer have to live as hopeless wanderers. We can live in a close relationship with Him. I would encourage you today to call upon Him and ask Him to forgive you of your sins.

347

DIVINE PROTECTION

And the Lord *God made clothing from animal skins for Adam and his wife.*
Genesis 3:21

God protects our efforts. God was there, even when Adam and Eve sinned and tried to cover their nakedness with fig leaves. When they sinned and made a bad decision, God covered them and took care of their needs.

If you've been living with the results of bad decisions, I want to encourage you to turn it over to the Lord and then forgive yourself. You don't have to walk around with shame and guilt over your head. Know that you are forgiven and that the Lord will cover your shame and guilt. You are not who you used to be. You are a new creation. All things have passed away; all things have become new.

348

INSTANT OBEDIENCE

On that very day Abraham took his son, Ishmael, and every male in his household, including those born there and those he had bought. Then he circumcised them, cutting off their foreskins, just as God had told him.

Genesis 17:23

In this passage, the Lord confirmed His covenant with Abraham by commanding him to circumcise himself and every male in his household. Abraham responded with instant obedience. He did not wait until the next day. He knew if he waited, he would probably talk himself out of it. The best time to respond to the Lord is immediately. The more you put it off, the more likely you'll talk yourself out of it. Don't delay, do it today!

JESUS WALKS WITH YOU

That same day two of Jesus' followers were walking to the village of Emmaus, seven miles from Jerusalem. As they walked along they were talking about everything that had happened. As they talked and discussed these things, Jesus himself suddenly came and began walking with them. But God kept them from recognizing him.

Luke 24:13-16

Jesus walks along with us in our disappointments. The disciples had just experienced a tremendous disappointment because Jesus had been crucified. They thought He would be the next king and deliverer of Israel. Jesus could have sent an angel or someone else to walk with them, but instead, He walked the entire seven miles with them from Jerusalem. This trip would have taken several hours. If you're disappointed today, you're not alone. Jesus is walking with you, and He's waiting to hear from you.

350

DON'T RETURN TO DEAD PLACES

Later, when he returned to Timnah for the wedding, he turned off the path to look at the carcass of the lion. And he found that a swarm of bees had made some honey in the carcass. He scooped some of the honey into his hands and ate it along the way. He also gave some to his father and mother, and they ate it. But he didn't tell them he had taken the honey from the carcass of the lion.
Judges 14:8-9

The Lord delivered Samson from a lion by helping him to kill it with his bare hands. Later, he returned to the carcass and found honey in it. He scooped some out, ate it, and gave some to his parents as well. He didn't tell his parents where he had found the honey because he had broken his Nazarite vow. From birth he had not touched a dead carcass or eaten anything from a dead carcass.

Unfortunately, Samson chose to go back to a place in his life from which God had already delivered him. In his arrogance, he thought he could handle the temptation. Instead, he went back to a dead place in his life. He sacrificed the anointing on his life at the expense of his flesh. Don't sacrifice your future for a momentary sweet tooth.

351

SUCCESS AND HUMILITY

*But when he had become powerful, he also became proud, which led to his
downfall. He sinned against the LORD his God by entering the sanctuary of the
LORD's Temple and personally burning incense on the incense altar.*
2 Chronicles 26:16

Success without humility breeds destruction. Humility attracts the favor
and blessings of God on your life. We must be careful because when God
begins to bless our lives, we can easily think it is because of something we
did. As leaders, we must develop humility. Consider these five ways to
develop humility:

- Admit you don't have all the answers.
- Admit it when you make a mistake.
- Seek godly counsel from others.
- Deflect praise from yourself to God and to others.
- Give credit to where credit is due in your life.

Be careful! The most dangerous time in your life is when you're most
successful. A spirit of humility will keep you grounded.

352

DON'T DEFEND YOURSELF

Shadrach, Meshach, and Abednego replied, "O Nebuchadnezzar, we do not need to defend ourselves before you."
Daniel 3:16

It's best not to answer your critics. When the three Hebrew boys faced persecution and criticism from those around them, they refused to respond in anger and instead left their case to the Lord. Likewise, when Jesus was brought before Pilate, He didn't try to take up His own case. He was confident that the Advocate, the Holy Spirit, would help Him and give Him the words to say. When facing persecution or criticism, our tendency is to fire back a quick response. When we refuse to answer our critics, we allow God to come to our defense, and He's never lost a case!

AFTER THE FURNACE

Then the king promoted Shadrach, Meshach, and Abednego to even higher positions in the province of Babylon.
Daniel 3:30

Before Shadrach, Meshach, and Abednego were promoted, they endured the furnace. Everyone wants to be promoted, few people want to be tested. Promotion follows great testing in your life. If you're enduring great testing today, then be encouraged because your promotion follows your testing.

354

SUDDEN STORMS

Then Jesus got into the boat and started across the lake with his disciples.
Suddenly, a fierce storm struck the lake, with waves breaking into the boat. But
Jesus was sleeping.
Matthew 8:23-24

The disciples were obeying the voice of God in their life, but they still ended up facing a storm. If we aren't careful, we can get a false impression that those who walk in obedience have a carefree and problem-free life. That's the furthest from the truth. Regardless of who you are, storms have a way of sneaking up on you and coming out of nowhere. It would be nice if God warned you about storms, but He usually doesn't. He just promises to be with you in the boat.

While the disciples were panicking, Jesus was sleeping. Jesus was sleeping because He was sovereign over all creation. In fact, He was the one who spoke creation into existence, and it was subject to His commands. In the end, He got up and rebuked the storm. Sometimes He rebukes the storms; other times, He rides them out with us.

355

TELL THE TRUTH

Looking at the man, Jesus felt genuine love for him. "There is still one thing you haven't done," he told him. "Go and sell all your possessions and give the money to the poor, and you will have treasure in heaven. Then come, follow me."
Mark 10:21

Sometimes the most loving thing you can do with someone is to tell them the truth. The truth hurts. Scripture reminds us that Jesus came with grace and truth (John 1:17). The best way to dispense truth is with a heaping of grace! Jesus loved the rich young ruler enough to tell him the truth.

356

ALL YOU CAN DO

She has done what she could and has anointed my body for burial ahead of
time.
Mark 14:8

Some disciples were incensed that the woman had "wasted" all the perfume and poured it on Jesus' head. More than likely, it was her inheritance or her marriage dowry. It was probably all that she had.

When the woman came to Jesus, she wanted to do something special for Him. She chose to give what she could. She couldn't give what she didn't have. It's easy to beat yourself up for not having more to give. Don't fall into this trap. Jesus sees your offering, and He knows it's the best you can do. If you do the best you can do, then He'll do the best He can do. The good news is that His best is always better than our best! You cannot out give God!

PAY ATTENTION!

"So pay attention to how you hear. To those who listen to my teaching, more understanding will be given. But for those who are not listening, even what they think they understand will be taken away from them."
Luke 8:18

Be careful what you listen to. What you listen to shapes your thoughts, and your thoughts become your life. Few people take the time to filter what they listen to, including music, people, TV shows, and other forms of entertainment. When you don't know what you want, anything will do.

Just because someone has a voice, doesn't mean they should be heard. Also, just because people are loud, doesn't mean you should listen to them. The crowd shouted for Barabbas when they should have been asking for Jesus.

358

ONE THING YOU NEED

But the Lord said to her, "My dear Martha, you are worried and upset
over all these details! There is only one thing worth being concerned
about. Mary has discovered it, and it will not be taken away from her."
Luke 10:41-42

In a world of busyness and distractions, it's easy to find ourselves worried and upset. Rarely does life go according to our plans.

Over the years, I've learned that the best thing I can do is spend time with Jesus. As I take time to sit at His feet, He has a way of making the rest of my day better. At the end of the day, the only thing we can take to heaven with us is our personal relationship with Jesus. Nothing more, nothing less. He's the one thing you need.

WEAR EYE PROTECTION

"Your eye is like a lamp that provides light for your body. When your eye is healthy, your whole body is filled with light. But when it is unhealthy, your body is filled with darkness."
Luke 11:34

If you've ever used power tools or operated lawn equipment, the first thing you'll notice is a small label that reads, "Wear eye protection." We obviously know this is to protect our eyes from damage. If we are honest, though, few people take heed to protect their eyes.

Your eyes allow you to see, but they also serve as the gateway to your spirit. If what you consume with your eyes is healthy, then your spirit will be healthy. If your visual consumption is unhealthy, your spirit will be unhealthy. If you don't like who you are, then you need to change what you consume. You are what you consume!

FEED YOURSELF

Humans can reproduce only human life, but the Holy Spirit gives birth
to spiritual life.
John 3:6

What you feed grows; what you starve dies. That's a law of nature, as well as a spiritual law. If you don't like what you have, you must change what you do. You can't keep sowing to your flesh and expect it to not affect your life. If you want to reap more of the Spirit, you need to do things that nourish and grow your spirit. This means praying, reading your Bible, listening to sermons, and being a part of a local church.

A DIVIDED PEOPLE

So the crowd was divided about him.
John 7:43

The mention of Jesus' name in our society brings all sorts of reactions. Some people love Him, while others despise Him. It was no different in Jesus' day.

Not everyone around you is going to be as excited as you are about Jesus. That's okay. Don't change your beliefs or your worship just because someone doesn't believe as you do. Our job is to be witnesses and to share our faith with others. We can't choose other people's responses. We can only choose to love people.

362

STAY CLOSE

Remain in me, and I will remain in you. For a branch cannot produce fruit if it is severed from the vine, and you cannot be fruitful unless you remain in me.
John 15:4

A few days ago, I was doing some yard work. I had to cut back some branches from a couple of overgrown trees. I cut them back and put the branches by the road to be picked up for removal. A couple of days later, I was walking around in my backyard, and I noticed that all the branches that had been cut had already started wilting and turning brown. I was honestly surprised as to how quickly they deteriorated. When they got separated from the vine, they lost their source of life. Branches were never designed to flourish apart from the rest of the tree. Likewise, we were never designed to flourish apart from our Creator. The key to a fruitful life is staying attached to the vine. The vine is Jesus, and all that we need for life, we can draw from Him.

YOU ARE NOT CONDEMNED

So now there is no condemnation for those who belong to Christ Jesus. And because you belong to him, the power of the life-giving Spirit has freed you from the power of sin that leads to death.
Romans 8:1-2

If you are a believer in Jesus Christ, you don't have to walk around feeling condemned and shamed for your past sins. Christ paid the price for your sins, and Scripture reminds us that "He has removed our sins as far from us as the east is from the west" (Psalm 103:12). Since you can't measure how far the east is from the west, they are no longer there.

If you're feeling shame or guilt from your past, it's not the Holy Spirit. Those feelings only come from Satan, who wants to accuse you before God. God has already forgiven you through Jesus Christ. When Satan reminds you of your past, remind Satan of his future!

364

AND AGAIN...

*But after a while the Philistines returned and again spread out across the valley of Rephaim. And again David asked the L*ORD *what to do. "Do not attack them straight on," the L*ORD *replied. "Instead, circle around behind and attack them near the poplar trees."*
2 Samuel 5:22-23

The enemy is relentless in his pursuit to destroy your life. David had just been crowned the new king of Israel and had just conquered Jerusalem. The enemy came knocking on David's door during what should have been a time of celebration.

If the enemy can't destroy your life, he'll surely attempt to disrupt your blessings. Don't be surprised when the enemy throws something at you during a time of celebration or right after a breakthrough. He's just mad at the favor and blessing of God on your life.

NEVERTHELESS

Nevertheless, that time of darkness and despair will not go on forever. The land of Zebulun and Naphtali will be humbled, but there will be a time in the future when Galilee of the Gentiles, which lies along the road that runs between the Jordan and the sea, will be filled with glory.

Isaiah 9:1

This verse is a promise that God spoke to Isaiah for Israel. Specifically, it promised the Messiah would go to Galilee of the Gentiles and fill it with his glory. The problem was that Israel was going through an Assyrian invasion. The nation of Israel was in between miracles, and they were enduring a season of darkness and despair.

Maybe you're going through a season of darkness and despair. This verse is a reminder that Jesus will come into your situation, and you will see his glory. In spite of your circumstances, God is in control of every season of your life. His Son will intervene in your life, and His promises still stand. This season will not go on forever!

ABOUT THE AUTHOR

Eric Speir is a serial encourager, writer, pastor, and bible college instructor. His goal is to help people get to know Jesus better. Eric holds a doctor of ministry degree in leadership development and creative communication. He and his wife, Roshelle, have four children and live near Atlanta, Georgia.

You can find out more information about Eric and his other writing projects through his blog at www.ericspeir.com.

If this book ministered to you in some way we would love for you to leave a review on Amazon! You can also email us at Eric@ericspeir.com.